I0786345

Philippine Demonological Legends and Their Cultural Bearings

MAXIMO D. RAMOS

PHOENIX PUBLISHING HOUSE
927 Quezon Avenue, Quezon City

Contents

Preface   vii

From the Publisher   xi

The Demons
   The Man Who Rode a Tikbalang   2
The Dragons
   The Woodcutter and the Python   20
The Dwarfs
   The Girl Who Stumbled at the School Gate   34
The Elves
   Letters from and to Frank   50
The Ghouls
   The Tuba Gatherer and the Corpse Thief   64
The Giants
   Angngalo and Aran   78
The Merfolk
   The Maiden and the Merman   94
The Ogres
   The Scold and the Ogre   110
The Vampires
   The Taxi Dancer Who Took Off at Midnight   128
The Viscera Takers
   The Manananggal at a Teachers' Conference   140
The Werebeasts
   Sometimes a Dog   152
The Witches
   A Varied Switching   164

Preface

THE PHILIPPINES is the world's major exporter of scientifically trained medical doctors to the United States, while folk healers continue to have extensive practice back home, prescribing cures to appease demonological beings whose domain, they say, the patient has violated. At twilight the healer casts uncooked rice or puts a bowl of saltless boiled chicken where the patient last worked or played before becoming ill. The healer then begs the spirits to accept the offering, forgive the patient's trespass, and heal him.

The farmer also offers rice cakes, cigars or cigarettes, wine—and now bottled carbonated drinks have become acceptable as well—before plowing his field and on the last day of harvest. These are the farmer's traditional rent on the land, for the folk believe that the usually invisible dwarfs in the area are the real owners of the land, the farmer who works it being just their tenant though it is titled to him.

Our parks should be decorated with figures of these ancient deities rather than with those of European fairies with butterfly wings and sharp-eared dwarfs with red or blue bonnets alien to Philippine folklore. Our gardens should contain figures of the creatures which our villagers tell legends about. Another appropriate project would be to place figures of these beings in our museums and perhaps on the outer walls of our churches as well. Solomon Saprid's sculpture of a man trying to subdue a *tikbalang* stands at the Makati Commercial Center complex, and Carlos V. Francisco's mural at the main lobby of the Philippine General Hospital shows a ferocious weredog. Figures of some of these faded gods on the outer walls of our churches would counterpoint the holy images inside and correspond to the gargoyles that serve as waterspouts on the roof edges of majestic medieval European cathedrals which no one has ever been heard to complain as being out of place. To the possible objection that children are more attracted to representations of these creatures than are adults and may remain outside looking at them instead of getting in, the reply is that the clergy should make their proceedings interesting enough to draw them in.

Some of the beliefs about these creatures may have been forgotten. But the kinds of behavior they shaped persist, especially where they serve to reinforce existing behavior patterns. Filipinos in hotel lobbies or aboard planes bound for international conferences can easily be spotted by their noise. This behavior pattern was probably born of the old belief that certain types of aswang descended on gatherings such as wakes for the dead and could be kept safely distant by the noise of those gathered near the dead. One should also be more understanding toward Filipinos who habitually spit in public places. The habit originated from the old habit of chewing betel leaves with lime and areca nut and spitting out the resulting fluid that was traditionally thought to drive off demonological beings. The unsightly habit of urinating in parks and at roadsides is also due to the belief that the salt in urine is thought effective in keeping demonological beings away.

Beliefs in these creatures also help explain the Filipino's love of spicy, salty, and sour foods. Our school gates are crowded with peddlers of these foods that nutritionists vainly rail against.

The Filipino's lack of experience in living in groups

larger than the family or the immediate neighborhood is
a consequence of the fact that his ancient gods had no
social organizations such as the Greco-Roman and
Scandinavian gods, for example, had.

The assertion often made by the Spanish writers of
sucesos to the effect that the Filipinos worshipped the
spirits of their ancestors is without basis in fact. These
so-called ancestral spirits were demons, dwarfs, and
elves instead.

Retold to start off each chapter here is a legend
about the category of Philippine lower mythological
being the chapter is about. As folklorists define them,
legends differ from folktales—traditional narratives told
to entertain or give lessons in acceptable behavior, while
legends are traditional stories which both those who tell
and those who hear them are ready to swear as having
actually happened.

Each introductory legend is followed by a more
extended comment on the cultural dimensions and
related aspects of the beliefs about the legendary being.

MAXIMO D. RAMOS, the first editor in chief of Phoenix Publishing House, was associated with the company from 1963 until his death on December 12, 1988. As editor and consultant, he gathered together a team of teachers who were creative, understood the needs of Filipino students, knew their pedagogy, and, above all, were committed to the ideals of nationhood espoused by my father, Dr. Ernesto Y. Sibal.

The present leadership of Phoenix Publishing House in the textbook field in all subject areas on all three levels of the educational system is due, in a large measure, to the unfaltering loyalty and passion for work of Dr. Ramos.

Dr. Ramos never relaxed his own personal pursuit of the Muse and continued to write short stories, poems, and essays. At the same time, he devoted special attention to serious research on Philippine mythology and folklore. All these were done as he taught and performed administrative duties at the Philippine Normal College and later at the University of the East.

Phoenix Publishing House takes pride in publishing these ten volumes of the essential works of Dr. Ramos. We know that his legacy will fire the imagination of Filipino students and inspire them to know more about their own folkways and folklore and to write them down for others to enjoy and appreciate. Dr. Ramos's only limitation perhaps is access to Filipino language as medium of his literary output. But he has shown the Filipino student that one can master the English language and use it to advantage in portraying Philippine reality. And because the setting is Filipino and the experiences are part of the Filipino tradition, we know that his writings will appeal to children and to adults as well.

His works, collectively titled REALMS OF MYTHS AND REALITY, consist of the following:

    I.   TALES OF LONG AGO IN THE PHILIPPINES
   II.   PHILIPPINE MYTHS, LEGENDS,
       AND FOLKTALES
  III.   LEGENDS OF LOWER GODS
  IV.   THE CREATURES OF MIDNIGHT
   V.   THE ASWANG COMPLEX
       IN PHILIPPINE FOLKLORE
  VI.   PHILIPPINE DEMONOLOGICAL LEGENDS
       AND THEIR CULTURAL BEARINGS
 VII.   BOYHOOD IN MONSOON COUNTRY
VIII.   PATRICIA OF THE GREEN HILLS
       AND OTHER STORIES
  IX.   REMEMBRANCE OF LENTS PAST
       AND OTHER ESSAYS
   X.   THE CREATURES OF PHILIPPINE
       LOWER MYTHOLOGY

This collection is our tribute to Dr. Maximo D. Ramos and our contribution to Filipiniana.

J. ERNESTO SIBAL
Publisher

The Demons

The Man Who Rode a Tikbalang

A YOUTH ONCE LIVED in a nipa hut on his farm outside
Pasig, just southeast of Manila. He had inherited the
fairly large farm as an only child, and he worked it
alone from sunrise to sunset-but could till only part of
it, the rest going to grass and reeds.

After an early supper he occasionally walked to
town, joined the boys at a small store there, and with.
them drank tuba, wine from the fermented sap of
trimmed coconut blooms. The boys would then smoke
and exchange stories, after which he would walk home
to bed.

He was on his way home under the stars one night
a month before the monsoon rains set in when, under a
tree beside the side road to his farm he saw a tall, dark
figure smoking a large cigar. He walked by the figure
without a word and wondered who it was.

No one was there the next time he walked to town.
But on his way home some nights later he saw the glow
of a cigar at the same spot. He put a cigarette to his
lips, walked to the smoker, and asked him for a light.
The smoker's cigar briefly glowed brighter and the cigar
was handed to him, and he glimpsed a dark stallion's
head with the hands, arms, shoulders, and chest of a
man. It was a *tikbalang*.

He had heard that if one was brave and snatched

two or three hairs from the mane of a tikbalang, wound them around his fingers, and mounted the creature, it would give him a marvelous ride across the sky, safely bring him right back home, and be his faithful servant.

The man snatched several strands from the mane of the creature, quickly twined them around his finger, and sprang to its back.

It reared and went off like a shot, and he held tight to its scruff while it increased its speed. Soon they had taken off the ground and were soaring over the town and the countryside. In a few moments the creature and its daring rider were over the mountains and the sea. The earth was distant and dim, and the stars were bright and the moon shone big. The ride was smooth, and the man enjoyed it immensely.

At last the tikbalang made a final burst of soaring and then headed back to earth. The river came into view and the dim town lights grew bright as the tikbalang banked and came to a gentle stop right at the foot of the man's ladder. He got off and tapped the creature's shoulder, and it trotted off into the night. Then he got up his ladder, opened the door, and went to bed relishing the thought of his delightful ride.

Thoughts of the ride raced through his head all through the next day, but he told no one about it.

He was on his way home from the store in town a few nights later when he saw the creature standing at the same spot. He had heard that if a tikbalang became your friend, it would plow and harrow your field, plant your crops, and be your faithful servant. He now led the creature to his tool shed and hitched it to his plow. It pulled the plow down the middle of his field and then went back and forth in a widening swath, going so fast that the man grew a little dizzy and went to bed hoping that his plow would last long enough to finish the job.

He woke up next morning to find his entire field, including the wide area that had lain idle all those years, plowed under, the moist clods gleaming in the morning sun.

He found the tikbalang standing quietly at the foot of his ladder when he went down the next evening. He hitched it to his harrow, and his field lay flat and smooth when he got up from bed the next morning.

He then laid out sacks of seed rice, and at night the tikbalang came, made seedbeds, and sowed the seed rice in them.

The seeds germinated, and in a month the seedlings were ready for transplanting. The tikbalang came one night soon after and transplanted them into the waiting field, and the entire field lay yellowish-green with the seedlings next morning, except for the slightly elevated patch around his hut where he raised greens and a few chickens for his table.

The rice grew, bore panicles, and headed, and he set scarecrows here and there in the field to keep the sparrows away.

Soon the rice was ready to reap, and the tikbalang came back one night and reaped the grain, and it had left it tied in neat sheaves by morning.

The man then spread mats and placed a heap of empty sacks next to the sheaves, and the following morning he found the grain threshed and placed in the sacks.

He spread mats made from palm leaves beside the
full sacks of unhulled rice, and the rice had been spread
on the mats lying in the sun to dry next morning. He
woke up early next day to find the rice hulled and in
neat sacks.

The man made a handsome profit from the sale of
his harvest to the traders who came for it.

The growing, reaping, hulling, and selling of rice
went on from year to year, and the man prospered. He
did not sell his carabao, for he sometimes harnessed it
to his cart and drove it to town and bought his household needs.

He built himself a more comfortable house, courted
a nice girl in the village, and wed her. He did not let
her know that he went out riding into the sky on the
back of the tikbalang on some evenings. But she knew
about his trips to town in the evenings now and then
for a smoke and a drink of coconut-juice wine and an
exchange of tales and jokes with the other boys. She
was pleased to learn that he had a faithful friend who
came to plow and harrow his field, sow the seed rice,
transplant the seedlings when they were ready, harvest
the grain, thresh and dry it in the sun, hull it, and
finally left it in rows of clean rice in sacks ready to sell.

THE TIKBALANG belongs to a category of legendary
beings known in the West as demons. The creature's
reported ability to rise into the air and fly or even just
glide without wings indicates either the early Filipinos'
lack of knowledge of aerodynamics or indeed their
intimations of jet propulsion.

The tikbalang is generally described as a tall, bulky,
and dark-complexioned being. Like other Philippine
demons he is commonly harmless and may indeed be
helpful. Tikbalangs are nevertheless much feared by
Philippine folk. They are said to live in large trees with
round or ovoid leaves, particularly the *kalumpang* (*Sterculia foetida* L.)and the *balete* (*Ficus balete* Merr.) The former
is known to the Iloko as *bañgar* and to the Visayans as

bubog. The unpleasant smell of kalumpang blooms can be nauseating, but the folk leave it alone and the tree is often the only piece of vegetation in an area. The Zambales Negritos call the kalumpang *takang demonio* (demon's excrement) because of the unpleasant smell of its flowers.

Unlike the European demons, the Philippine demons do not have pointed ears, have neither horns nor fangs, and in at least one case are without a head.

The local names of Philippine demons, together with the names of the Philippine ethno-linguistic groups that tell legends about them, are:

allawig—Iloko
anggitay—Tagalog
ani-ani—Zambale
bangungot—Tagalog
bantay, baras—Pangasinense
binangenan—Dumagat
kapre—Bikol, Iloko, Tagalog
lagtaw—Tausog
mutya—Iloko, Cuyonon, Tagalog

pugot—Iloko, Pangasinense
santilmo—Iloko, Tagalog, Visayan
silew-silew—Pangasinense
talahiang—Chabakano
tikbalang—Tagalog
tulung, tuwung—Zambales Negrito

The word *demon* is from the Greek *daimon*, which refers to a supernatural being or spirit below the rank of a god. The word originally had both a good and a bad connotation. Socrates was believed to have a daimon, a familiar spirit which gave him a warning when he was about to decide wrong. In primitive societies, good and bad spirits are not clearly distinguishable since the benevolent spirits are sometimes maleficent, and unfriendly spirits can be made beneficent after the proper rites are performed.

Demons are generally evil spirits, however, and can move fast. European demons generally had the shape of animals and birds or were in the form of goblins in male or female shapes. In East Asia are found many kinds of hostile demons. The *rakshashas*, for example, can quickly take a wide variety of shapes and have great strength.

The evil demons—the *kuei*—among the Chinese made the night hours fearsome. They crowded around homes and along roads at night. They feared light, however, and fled to their places of hiding with the rise of the sun.

The Filipinos' use of noise and fire to scare demons away came from the Chinese, who use bonfires, candles, torches, and particularly fireworks to frighten the kuei off and by use of these cleanse their homes and communities on New Year's Day. These beliefs are the source of the noise Filipinos make with fireworks, bamboo cannon, and firearms on New Year's Eve.

Miguel Simera, 90, of Batangas City, told Juanita H. Mendoza, a teacher and researcher, that he was walking home late one night when he saw a man in white seated under a tree and smoking. He greeted the man, took a cigarette out of his pocket, and asked for a light. The man did not answer but ran away instead, and Simera only heard the man's heavy footsteps in the bamboo grove he went through. Simera hurried home.

Lorenzo Noriega, 75, of Pinamukhan, Batangas City, told researcher Mendoza about his late grandfather's two encounters with a tikbalang. After supper one evening, the family sat in the sitting room when a great uncle came asking for corn. The grandfather told him to go to the cornfield for them and he would follow. The brother left and he followed and saw his brother cutting down every corn plant he passed by, big and small. He told the brother to cut down only those with mature fruit, but the brother became angry and soon the two brothers were fighting. The grandfather was about to overcome the younger man but the latter leaped into the air three times and overcame him and then leaped into a nearby stream. The older man fortunately got hold of the branch of an *ayungan* tree beside the stream and did not fall into the deep water. The other suddenly left, and he shouted to his wife, who asked the menfolk in the neighborhood to go to the cornfield and find him. They found him by the stream. His real brother came next day and said he had never come around asking for corn. They then knew that a tikbalang had come instead.

Another Pinamukhan account says that Noriega was plowing his field one day. He did not notice that the sun had set. He unyoked the cow from his plow and sent it on the way home as he had often done before. He soon followed and on the way he met his father who asked him why he was going home so late. They walked on home together.

At home his wife wondered why the cow had come home without him. She waited and waited, and about ten o'clock she asked the menfolk in the neighborhood to help her go and find him. They went to look for him in the field but did not find him. Finally they went down to a stream and saw him there. They took him home and he kept insisting that he be allowed to get out though the windows and door had been bolted.

Finally he realized that it was close to midnight and that the man he met was not his father but a tikbalang. It had made him lose his sense of time and direction.

Miguel Siscar, of San Luis, Batangas, told teacher-researcher Rosalinda S. Holgado that there was a scarcity of water in Barrio Muzon, in San Luis, and he got up to go and fetch water from a place called Rigin, in San Luis, at 3:00 AM The morning was cold and he wanted to light a cigarette but had forgotten to bring a match. He met a large and tall man wearing a hat as wide as a washerwoman's vat and smoking a cigar as large as a man's leg. Undaunted, he asked the stranger to let him light his cigarette on his cigar and the giant let him do so. The glow of the giant's cigar was so bright that the surroundings were lighted. The man thanked the giant and walked on. The giant was no longer there when he looked back after taking three steps. The local folk later told him that the creature lived in a large rock by the road to a river leading to Taal Lake. They added that the creature harmed no one who showed respect to it.

The *allawig*, also known as *silew-silew* ('lighter'), is a ball of fire moving across open fields or through wooded areas at night. Unlike fire, it ignites nothing it touches. It is commonly red but may be blue, green, orange, or yellow. Unlike a real flame, too, it is round rather than peaked. It may burn bright or just flicker. One under its spell follows it and is then led round and round until he falls down in exhaustion. The creature may also lead a man into a mudhole or swamp where he can drown. One under the spell of the allawig should take off his clothes and put them on inside out. The creature will then leave and he will find his way home, which may prove to be just around the corner after all.

The *anggitay* was reported from Santo Tomas, Batangas, by the late Aproniano G. Castillo, a lawyer and the
father of this writer's daughter-in-law, Exaltacion C.
Ramos, a psychologist. It has a peculiar anatomy. Seen
from in front, it is a beautiful maiden from head to foot,
and it is a haggard mare seen from behind. It sits in a
tree in a wood and quietly watches wayfarers go by.

The *ani-ani* is said to stand eighteen feet tall. A man
may think he is standing between two trees and then
realize that he is between the lower legs of the ani-ani.
The creature lumbers along because of its great size. It
is dark-complexioned, hairy, and bearded. Its nose is
flat and its mouth wide, and it has a rough skin. It
generally appears when there is a new moon and may
be seen at night smoking on the branch of a large tree
beside a country road such as the *bulala* (Iloko) or *talisay*
(Tagalog) (*Terminalia catappa* L.) The leaves of this tree
turn autumn red toward the end of the year, and the
Americans had them planted around the town squares
throughout the archipelago soon after they arrived in
order to induce the people to gather and socialize there.

But demons were soon reported to frequent those trees
and scared the folk away instead. The trees have since
been cut down.

The ani-ani blocks the path of a wayfarer at night. It
changes its shape from that of a tall, dark man to that
of a carabao without horns, a horse, or a hog and back
into a tall, dark man again.

The *bangungot*, believed in by the Tagalog, is identi-
cal with the *batibat* of the Iloko. It is often blamed for
the death of partygoers who eat and drink to excess.
Filipino laborers who were shipped to the canefields of
Hawaii in the 1920s and died of nightmares after they
ate and drank excessively were said to be the victims of
the bangungot. The creature is reported to be as large
around the waist as a sack of rice and to live in a cavity
in a house post where it resided before the post was cut
down as a tree in the forest and has continued to inhabit that cavity. It sits on a person who goes to sleep
beside the post. Whoever the creature sits on cannot
breathe because of its enormous weight and because it
is said to stuff its penis in his mouth and its testicles in

his nostrils, and the victim then suffocates. It is said to be futile to scream when a bangungot is sitting on one. Instead, one should bite one's own thumb and wiggle one's big toe. Village folk avoid sleeping beside house posts for fear of the bangungot that may be in a concealed cavity in the post. In European folklore, beautiful women in the form of nightmares are said to similarly strangle those in bed by making love to them and then suffocating them in their embrace.

The *bantay* resembles an old man. It sits in a tree and turns into a white rooster that grows bigger and bigger and then smaller and smaller before the beholder's eyes. It resides in large trees beside streams and usually appears under a new moon, particularly in a drizzle. As a little boy, this writer used to hear of a white rooster and a black hen with many chicks that went down a tree in the town at night, walked along the street for a block-and-a-half, and then went up another tree on the same street without making a single sound.

The *baras* is a forest-dwelling demon in Pangasinan. It is known as *kirbas* to the Iloko and *kalariot* to the Pampango. It is tall, dark, and ugsome. It enters a village at night, opens an unbolted door or window in a home where a pretty girl is asleep, and gets in. It then picks her up and carries her off to its abode in the woods. When she wakes up and sees him, she may become insane from fright.

The word *kapre* is commonly used by all the Hispanized Philippine groups and is today the most widely used name for demons in the country. The Filipinos dropped their local names for the demons in favor of the Spanish name after the Spanish contact. Ismael Rameillah, a cultural attache in the Arab Emirates office in Manila, told this writer that an unconverted man is called *cafr* by his people. The Spaniards, whose country was occupied by the Muslim Moors, known as *Moros* in Spanish, for over 800 years, called the creatures *cafre* and evidently applied the term to equivalent creatures

they heard about from the Filipinos when they arrived
in the country in the sixteenth century. The term
became *kapre* to the Filipinos, whose languages lack the
labio-dental /f/. A kapre is said to grow taller and then
shorter and back again to normal size before the
beholder's eyes. It is also reported to have the nauseating smell of a goat—*cabra* in Spanish—and hence there
may have been a transfer of meanings in this case after
the Spaniards got here because of the similarity in
sounds.

The kapre can assume the shape of a carabao or a
large cat, dog, or hog. For this reason, the Ibanags call
the creature *ammalabi* ('the ever-changing'). Its dark skin
is hairy and coarse, and it has large eyes and ears and
thick lips. Its eyes are said to be the size of saucers, and
it has a low nose and a large mouth. It commonly
appears under a new moon, particularly when it is
drizzling.

It is reported to frequent large abandoned buildings
in towns and cities. A kapre is reported to have inhabited the fairly large old trees lining Legarda Street, in
downtown Manila, before these were recently cut down.
A kapre is also reported to haunt the Aguinaldo shrine
in Kawit, Cavite.

A kapre may be seen seated in a large tree early in
the evening, a big cigar glowing in its mouth. The cigar
is said not to grow shorter while the kapre smokes it.
One who sees a kapre and is brave enough should lasso
it with a strong rope and tie the rope to the tree. One
will find the end of the rope sunk in the ground next
morning. If one quietly digs there, one will find a jar of
gold, but the gold will turn to ashes if anyone sees him
digging for it or carrying it home.

Artemio Asuelo, whose house stands close to several
bamboo clumps just around the corner from where this
is being written, says that two of his sons were driving
home on a carabao cart from his farm in Bangar one
evening when they saw a twelve-foot giant Negro
trying to overtake them while they were passing by a

bangar tree. One of them jumped off the back of the carabao and ran home in terror, while the other helplessly stayed in the cart while it sped behind the carabao hitched to it since its halter was beyond his reach.

Hilarion Belloso, a truck mechanic and tinsmith, once owned a reconditioned weapons carrier with which he hired himself out to thresh rice, driving over the panicles back and forth several times to dislodge the grains from the rice heads. He and his man drove out to the open field behind Asuelo's house to pick up a load of rice to thresh one evening when they saw a large man squatting beside a pile of straw stacked up to dry before being stored to feed livestock during the lean months. The man was as tall on his haunches as a man on his feet. The two men went back for two additional loads to check and found that it was indeed a kapre. They then drove home without a word except to say that they would return to finish the job next day.

There are legends about the *mutya* from all over the country. Among the Cuyonon of Palawan, the creature is known as *moya,* a word derived from the Sanskrit *muya* ('jewel'). The creature is said to resemble a live coal the size of one's thumb and to be the plaything of the kapre. The late Francisco Armullas, a former road worker from San Antonio, Zambales, told this writer that a mutya occasionally appeared in his backyard at the edge of town on dark nights. It would slowly rise counterclockwise around a bamboo post of his backyard trellis, and it glowed bright enough to show the circle of amorphous roots around each node in the bamboo post. It then quietly bounded across the backyard and vanished in an acacia tree where a kapre was known to reside. Armullas added that it was perhaps the same kapre and its mutya that sometimes appeared in his backyard where he formerly lived outside the town, and both followed when his family moved into their new location. He also said that to catch a mutya, one should cast the lid of a clay pot over it and then reach in for it beneath the rim of the lid. Whoever possessed a mutya is said to have the strength of ten, but Armullas said he had never tried catching the mutya in his backyard, for it belonged to his kapre friend which, whenever the demon, clad in fatigues, walked silently behind him when he went out lantern fishing at night in the rice fields during the rainy season, he would return home with his hip basket full of fish. He added that the kapre looked into his house through an open window one dark night to say that a typhoon was due to come. A typhoon did soon come and would have made off with the sidings of his house if he had not reinforced the cords that tied them to the posts after the kapre's warning.

The *pugot* is said to be a tall, headless Negroid living in large trees with large rounded leaves, such as the bulala (Iloko) or *talisay* (Tagalog), mentioned earlier. It is said to be often attracted to pretty village maidens and stones the house where its human rival is seated with the girl it loves. It changes its size and shape to frighten the beholder and turns into a large, headless domestic animal. Fire is said to leap out of its open throat, but the creature is afraid of fire itself.

The *santilmo* is a ball of fire sometimes seen in open fields and in swamps. Its name is perhaps derived from *St. Elmo*, the ignis fatuus of Western folklore, beliefs about which European sailors probably introduced into the Philippines when they arrived. The creature bounces on the ground as it rolls off, and wayfarers who follow it will go around in circles and get lost. One in such a fix should sit down, take his clothes off, and put them on again inside out. Only then will he get his bearings and find his way home.

The demon known as *sarangay* to the Ibanag of the Cagayan Valley is tall and dark. It has coarse, long hair, and it wears large earrings. It lows like a bull and chases wayfarers at night. It possesses a magic jewel which glows in the dark. One brave enough to snatch the jewel from it and keeps it in his mouth will have the strength of ten.

The *talahiang* of the Zamboangans in the far South is over ten feet tall and is said to have coarse, dark, and kinky hair. Its lips are thick and it has large teeth in a large mouth. It may be seen sitting in a large tree after nightfall and makes wayfarers lose their way. A shout will send it scampering off in the form of a frightened monitor lizard.

The tikbalang told about in the legend this chapter starts with is not always helpful. It may assume the shape of a wayfarer's close relative and make him lose his way. Fr. Silverio Deltour, CICM, a Belgian priest who is the bursar of the Zambales Diocese, was once stationed in Pasig, the setting of the above legend. He recalls that on a field trip to Talim, a small but fertile island on Laguna de Bay, while his party were going through a thick growth of reeds, some of them yelled now and then to keep their companions informed about where they each were. They were told to be quiet or the tikbalang would hear them, assume the shape of an acquaintance, and pretend to lead them to the right path while in fact making them lose their way. The European will-o'-the-wisp is supposed to do that, too.

A daring tikbalang kidnapped one of the belles at a grand ball in old Manila on the night of April 15, 1580, or just nine years after the Spaniards captured the city from its Muslim founders. The creature was described as a "tall, hideous creature . . . in a dark tunic . . . its long straight hair flowing over its shoulders and with the wrinkled yellow feet of a bird." It had on a dark cloak which hung down to its knees, and its legs were those of a horse.

Tomas Ortiz, a seventeenth-century Augustinian priest in Central Luzon, griped that the tikbalang was giving him stiff competition. He said the Filipinos so feared the creature that "they come to make friends with him and surrender their rosaries to him and receive from him superstitious things such as hairs, stones, and other things, that they may be aided by him in certain of their affairs."

Lucetta K. Ratcliff wrote about the tikbalang for the
Journal of American Folklore in 1949: "They have bodies
like those of men, but their heads are similar to those of
horses. Their limbs are said to be so long that when
they sit their knees reach above their heads. When they
laugh, all you can see is mouth."

The *tulung*—or *tuwung*—of the Negritos at the foot
of Mt. Pinatubo, in Zambales, and the *binangenan* of the
Dumagat Negritos on the coast of Aurora, all the way
across Central Luzon, closely resemble the tikbalang.
The American anthropologist Robert B. Fox, discoverer
of the Tabon Cave Man, in Palawan, and thus pushed
the frontiers of Philippine prehistory by 50,000 years,
did field work for his Ph. D. dissertation for the University of Chicago on the culture of the Pinatubo Negritos
just after World War II. Fox described the tulung in
terms that identify it with the tikbalang. He wrote:
"This spirit is usually described as being horselike but
having clawed feet, long hair, and very large testicles."
Similarly, Damiana Amazona wrote that the binangenan
"looked somewhat like a horse, but there was fire in its
back from head to tail."

17

In Europe, human feces is sometimes called "the devil's signature" because that creature is said to smear doorknobs with it. Dr. Fox also reports that the Mt. Pinatubo Negritos call the kalumpang tree, with its tiny blooms that exude fecal smell and for that reason are pollinated by flies, takang demonio (demon's excrement), and how it ever came to get that name is rather puzzling.

With their widespread fear of demons, rural Filipinos customarily bolt their doors and windows at night. They wrap themselves from head to foot with cotton sheets or even warm woolen blankets when they go to bed though this gives them much discomfort in their tropical country. They keep away from trees at night and prefer to stay indoors rather than go out promenading in the dark. They let no large trees grow in their yards. When a Filipino buys a residential lot, the first thing he generally does is to cut down the trees on it. Or, fearful to cut them down, he digs pits under them and keeps slow fires burning there, casting animal hair, feathers, bovine hooves, horns, bones, and today rubber and plastic as well into them, since the acrid smell of these things is thought to keep demons away.

The Dragons

The Woodcutter and the Python

A MAN SLUNG the twine on his burden basket around his shoulder and tied his sheathed bolo to his waist. Then he picked up his axe and walked into the forest to cut down a tree to build his house with.

The woods grew darker with trees as he went. He stopped at the foot of a tree near a brook hard by which lay a fallen log. "Perhaps knocked down by a recent typhoon," he thought. Spiny rattan and other climbing vines draped the surrounding trees and obscured his view.

He put down his basket on the log and with his bolo cleared the vines standing in his way. He would fell the tree now, lop off its top and its branches, and next morning return with his water buffalo, a yoke, and rattan traces and pull the log home.

He started swinging his axe at the foot of the tree he had picked, pausing only now and then to catch his breath.

Halfway in his labors near noon, he tied his bolo to his waist and walked to a nearby brook. He gathered some snails there and picked a handful of tender fern shoots from the margin of the brook. Then he walked back to where he had camped. Into a small clay pot he poured three or four handfuls of rice grains out of a brown pouch he pulled out of his basket and put just enough water in it to go halfway up his middle finger when he stood that on top of the rice.

He then set three knee-size stones on the log to make a stove. He gathered some dry faggots, arranged a few of these in the fireplace, picked up a handful or two of dry moss, and put this where the faggots met under the pot. Then he struck his flint and soon had a lively fire burning under the pot.

He sat on the log to break the fern tips into short pieces and get them ready to boil with the snails and the salted fish he had also brought along in a small bamboo tube.

Then something happened. The log he was sitting and cooking on moved, almost knocking off the pot. "An earthquake," he thought, rearranging the faggots under the pot.

Next the log shook even harder. He looked up and saw the farther end of the log arching toward him, and he realized that what he had thought a log was a large python. It had been awakened by the fire on its back from its long sleep to digest the deer or wild hog it must have swallowed whole and it would have slept a whole month to digest it.

Too late he tried to dodge the monster's mouth as it descended on him. The python picked him up with its large teeth and swallowed him whole. He was swiftly pushed through the monster's gullet and was soon down in its stomach.

Struggling for breath, the man felt all over his body and was greatly relieved to find himself whole. Quickly he unsheathed his bolo on his waist, sliced his way out of the python's tough belly, and crawled out panting.

He looked and saw the great tail of the wounded monster swinging toward him, threatening to catch him in its coils and crush him in its powerful grip. He leaped behind a large tree, dodged the oncoming coils, and stumbled out of reach. He watched the bleeding monster slowly weaken and grow still.

The man picked up his things and hurried out of the woods. "I shall have to go elsewhere for a tree for my house," he said.

The Philippine dragons fall under four categories:
1. Birdlike dragons
    bawa —West Visayan
    laho —Pampango, Tagalog
    minokawa —Bagobo
2. Fishlike dragons
    bakunawa — West Visayan
3. Crocodile-like dragon
    buwaya —Iloko, Tagalog, etc.
4. Snakelike dragons
    bîlat—Iloko
    mameleu—West Visayan
    markupo—West Visayan
    sawâ—Tagalog

THE SNAKE in this folktale is a dragon—a fabular creature which in European folklore is a large reptile that breathes out fire. The dragon which Beowulf slew in the Anglo-Saxon epic was a large, fire-breathing water snake, while that killed by Sigfried in the German epic *Nibelungenlied* had a shoulder and was thus perhaps crocodile-like.

The myths of India abound in *nagas* and *naginis*—snake gods and goddesses with human heads and torsos who are often helpful to the gods and to humans as well.

In Sumerian mythology the god Marduk slays the dragon Tiamat, a fierce winged lion.

In East Asia the dragon consists of parts of various animals, too. There the dragon is believed to bring good fortune rather than suffering as in the West. It is considered a friendly creature—whence the merry dragon dances of China and Japan. The composite nature of the Chinese dragon is best shown in this terse description: "Its horns resemble those of a deer, its head that of a camel, its eyes those of a devil, its neck that of a snake, its claws those of an eagle, the scales of its feet those of a tiger, its ears those of an ox, but some have no ears, the organ of hearing being said to be in the horns of the creature" (E. T. C. Werner, *Myths and Legends of China*, New York, 1922). Werner adds that there are small dragons and large dragons, the small dragon being the size of a silkworm and the large dragon "fills the Heaven and the Earth. There are azure, scaly, horned, hornless, winged, etc., dragons. A horned dragon develops into a flying dragon in a thousand years."

The prehistoric Filipinos had extensive trade relations with the Chinese. There are many trade and culinary terms in Chinese in the Philippine languages. Prehistoric porcelain ware from China are held as treasures in homes in the hinterlands such as the Cordillera range in Northern Luzon and in Mindanao as well.

Like the Chinese dragons, the Philippine dragons have various animal shapes—snakes, crocodiles, and sharks—and like the Chinese dragon, some combine the features of various animals. They may be large or small, and they fall under four animal types. The first type are the birdlike dragons, such as Manaul, the eagle in the earliest recorded Philippine creation myth which Miguel de Loarca recorded in a book published in 1582. Ac-

cording to this myth, Manaul flew back and forth in the sky without rest because there was yet no land. He then made the sea and the sky fight, the sky dropping into the sea large rocks that stilled it and became the Philippine archipelago.

Other birdlike Philippine dragons are the *bawa* of the Hiligaynon in the Western Visayas and the *minokawa* of the Bagobo in Southeastern Mindanao.

There are also the fish-like *bakunawa* of the Hiligaynon, the saurian *buwaya* throughout the archipelago, and the snakelike *mameleu* and *markupo* of the Hiligaynon and the pythons *sawâ* of the Tagalog and the *biklat* of the Iloko.

A myth told by the Bagobo of Southeastern Mindanao to Laura Watson Benedict in 1913 said that the minokawa was a bird as large as the islands of Negros and Bohol—whether together or separately is not stated. Its beak and talons were made of steel, its eyes were mirrors, and its feathers were like sharp swords. It lived "outside the sky, at the eastern horizon." There it lay in wait for the moon and tried to

seize her in its mouth when she emerged from one of
eight holes in that part of the sky after her journey
under the earth. The moon had eight holes in the eastern horizon to come out of when rising and eight holes
in the western horizon to get into after traveling across
the sky. She feared the minokawa, for it tried to catch
her each day. It tried to grab her in its mouth just when
she came out of one of the holes in the east. The Bagobo were afraid that if the minokawa should succeed
in swallowing both the moon and the sun, it would
next come down to earth and devour the people.

The bawa, much feared by the Hiligaynon of the
Western Visayas, lived above the sky. They believed
that above the sky was a large cave called *calulundan*, its
entrance obscured by smoke, and in the cave dwelt the
dragon bird bawa.

Jose Maria Pavon y Aranguro wrote in 1839 that the
bakunawa which the West Visayans also feared had the
shape of a shark and its mouth was as large as a lake.
"Its tongue was very red, and about its mouth it had
whiskers about one *palmo* [open palm] in length." It had

large gray wings, powerful in flight. There were gills
and small wings at its sides—its multiple wings somewhat resembling the three pairs of wings the archangels
had in Milton's *Paradise Lost*. It occasionally swallowed
the sun or moon or both, causing much-feared eclipses.

The mameleu of Negros Island was a large sea
serpent. Its body was as large as that of a carabao and
was thirty fathoms long. Its eyes burned like torches. Its
head was the size of a carabao's, and two horns grew
on it. Its long tongue had thornlike hairs. Its tusks were
sharp and its tail was forked.

Everywhere in the Philippines the eclipsed sun or
moon is believed to be in the mouth of the sky dragon,
and the folk beat on drums and other noise-making
objects to panic the dragon into letting it go. When I
had occasion to speak on the subject at the Philippine
Normal College, in Manila, in the sixties, a young
American anthropologist doing field work in the area
rose to say that at the nearby Rizal Park he had recently
been puzzled to see Filipinos feverishly beating on
noise-makers such as pans and drums during an eclipse
of the sun.

Tomas Ortiz, another seventeenth-century Spanish
missionary in the Philippines, reported in his book
Practico del Ministerio that the Filipinos in various parts
of the country went out into the fields and streets and
beat on bells and other objects in an attempt to free the
moon during an eclipse.

The widespread Filipino practice of propitiating
crocodiles in the past arose from the Philipine belief
that these creatures were dragons. The seventh injunc-
tion of the Code of Kalantiao, published in 1433, states:
"They shall be put to death . . . who kill . . . the striated
crocodile." The early inhabitants of Negros Island,
where Kalantiao was a chief, revered the crocodile,
"especially if it be mottled and lives in deep water."

The missionary Juan de Plasencia arrived in the
Philippines in 1577 and labored among the Tagalog in
and around Lilio, Laguna, where he was to die and be

buried. In his *Los Costumbres de los Tagalos* (1589), he reported that the Tagalogs paid reverence to "the water lizards which they called *buwaya*," or crocodile, and feared them. He added that the natives customarily offered the crocodiles they passed by a portion of the meat they carried in their boats, throwing it into the water or putting it on the bank.

Franciso Colin, another early Spanish missionary in the country, reported in his book *Labor Evangelica* (1663) that the Filipinos "held the crocodile in the greatest veneration, and when they saw it in the water cried out, '*Nuno*,' meaning 'grandfather'. They begged it not to harm them and cast food to it in the water."

Jose Rizal was from the lakeside town of Calamba, Laguna, and habitually traveled by launch to Manila where he was to take his A.B. with highest honors from the Ateneo de Manila, then as now a leading institution of higher learning run by the Jesuits. He wrote that he had often seen the natives tossing food to crocodiles on the banks of the Pasig River and begging these creatures to have mercy on them.

Alfredo R. Roces, editor in chief of the ten-volume encyclopedia *Filipino Heritage*, likes to show off an elegant brass gong from Borneo engraved with a dragon swallowing the moon. One who looks at the newly-risen full moon on a clear night will see markings on its face. These, of course, are mountains and depressions, but the Philippine folk believe them to be the marks made by the teeth of the sky dragon which bites the moon during what astronomers know as eclipses, and they believe that the dragon can be panicked into releasing the moon by the noise they make on earth during an eclipse. The folk say that the eclipsed moon is red because it is bleeding from the dragon's bite, and the dragon will come down to earth and devour the people in turn unless it is made to let go of the moon.

The folk also believe that lightning flashes during a thunderstorm come from the fierce eyes of the sky dragon. They say that rolling thunder is the roar com-

ing from the folds of the dragon's elongated body.
Village folk still drape mirrors and sprinkle vinegar out
of their windows during a thunderstorm to keep the
sky dragon away.

An eclipse or even just a darkening of the sun or
moon by clouds is called *naglalahô* in Tagalog and
Pampango. The word is derived from *Rahu*, the name of
the Hindu god believed to occasionally manage to
engorge the sun or moon, causing an eclipse. The pho-
neme /r/ does not occur in Tagalog and other Philippine languages, whence the change from *Rahu* to *laho*.

An ancient clay artifact recently dug out of the
Calatagan area, on the Batangas coast, shows what is
probably a human soul crossing the sea on a crocodile-
shaped boat, perhaps into the afterlife.

Snakes are tolerated and even welcomed in Philippine granaries and homes. The widespread belief is that
snakes bring good luck and that rice stored in a granary
with a snake in it will last beyond the next harvest. It
may, of course, indeed last that long because the snake
keeps the rice free from rats and mice. Snakes are

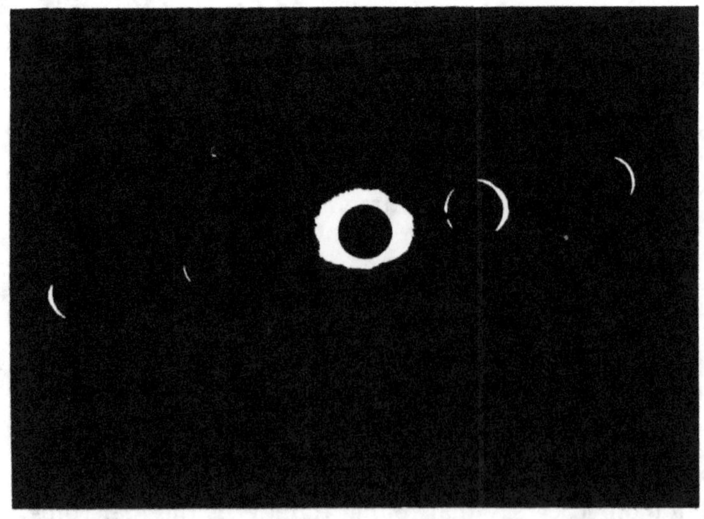

allowed in rural homes throughout the country, being said to bring good fortune. In the Visayas, geckos are welcome in homes for the same reason too, though in Luzon they are killed, for there the folk say that a gecko that sticks to one's skin can only be dislodged by being doused with salted-fish sauce or vinegar.

Children on the west coast of Luzon are still warned against the *bannagaw*, a legendary ferocious crested snake no one seems to have yet seen. They are also told to watch out for the *palapal* ('thrower'), said to be a two-headed snake that coils up and then casts itself at and fatally bites wayfarers. And they are told to fear the amphisbaena that, with a head on both ends, crawls back and forth with equal speed.

A barber from Botolan, a town adjacent to the most heavily wooded zone of Zambales, tells about a cattle man who one late afternoon entered his ranch at the edge of the forest to see why his stock were getting fewer instead of increasing. He walked inside the perimeter of his ranch to check his fence. In the failing light he saw what he thought a large darkened opening

in the fence next to the forest. Looking closer, he found
it to be the open mouth of an enormous python. Then
he knew that into it many of his cattle had walked
thinking it was an open gate.

This writer's son Romeo tells of a python some
thirty feet long and about two feet across its middle
which he once saw in a thick wood on the boundary of
Quirino and Aurora provinces, in Eastern Luzon, while
out hunting there with Ilongot head takers. The men
quietly walked away scared.

A myth which the Tagbanua Negritos of Palawan,
just north of Borneo, explains the origin of earthquakes.
It says that the world is supported by a single post
around which is coiled a large snake, Taliakuod, who
shakes the post, causing an earthquake, when displeased with the world's inhabitants. Taliakuod was a
dragon god. This myth somewhat resembles that illustrated by a Hindu miniature of the eighteenth century
now in the Musée Guimet in Paris. There the *devas* and
asuras, good deities and harmful deities, use the body of
the snake Vasuki, which is coiled around Mount Man-
dara to churn the sea. The mountain is borne on the
back of the god Vishnu in the form of a turtle so that
the whirling mountain will not sink into the sand
beneath the sea.

This writer's wife, Socorro, of San Antonio, Zambales, recalls that her father, Melanio Buenaventura, was
in 1916 the supervising teacher of the next town of San
Marcelino, twelve kilometres down a narrow road
across rice fields. Tired from his long day's work, he
was riding home half asleep on horseback early one
evening when, two hundred metres from the edge of
town, his horse suddenly neighed and reared. He
opened his eyes and saw a large python suspended
from a balete tree, evidently lying in wait for prey. He
whipped his horse and galloped away. Recently inter-
viewed, the elderly folk living in the area, which is still
separated from the town, said that where they now live
was sixty years ago a swamp where spiny maguey

hemp grew, and there a python denned. They added that the snake may have quietly left for the mountains across a river a kilometre south of the town when the swamp was filled to make a county road that now goes through the area. The python was perhaps considered a god by the local folk with the awe befitting it.

It is likely that the beliefs about dragons as snakes, saurians, or sharks later spilled over into beliefs about smaller creatures such as common snakes and lizards, and these have persisted to the present.

Conventional scholars held that Indian influences on Philippine culture have been religious and political in nature and that Chinese influence has been economic. What has just been said above would suggest that the Chinese influence has to some extent been of a religious nature as well.

In the above tale, if the python, being a god and therefore immortal, had not been killed, the account would be a legend, believed to be true by both the reconteur and the listener. But it is killed and thus, strictly speaking, the narrative is a folktale.

The Dwarfs

The Girl Who Stumbled
at the School Gate

A HIGH SCHOOL GIRL was about to enter the school gate
one morning when she stumbled. She quickly got up,
brushed off her dress, arms, and knees, and walked in.

She seemed all right at first but got home at the end
of the day complaining about pain in her back and
finding it hard to breathe.

Her father went for a healer, and the healer asked
her if anything unusual had recently happened to her.

She told him she had stumbled at the school gate, and
he rubbed alum on her arms, knees, and back and said
that she had stumbled on a *taong-lupa*—an invisible little
old man of the fields and shrubberies who had probably
gone near the schoolyard to listen and look.

The girl said she felt little pain and would need no
further attention next morning.

She and her group were doing an experiment in the
biology laboratory room a few days later when she saw
a little bald-headed old man walk in through the door.
He went to her without a word and tried to take the
ball pen she was writing with from her hand. "Come
out to the school yard with me," he said.

She was greatly annoyed and kicked him instead.
She told no one about the incident, however. "It's nice
to have a little secret," she thought. "And besides, no
one will believe what I say about the little man."

But her foot soon ached. She told her mother about
it when her mother got home from the office in the
evening, and her mother put her in bed and told her to
rest and would probably feel better next morning.

The little old man entered her room soon after dark.
She was annoyed and yelled at him to leave, and he left
without a word.

Her mother heard her raised voice. She entered the

room and found her in a trance. Her cheeks were flushed and her eyes unseeing.

Her father went to fetch a healer who lived in a small hut across the river early next morning. He came and asked for five strong men to hold the girl since she was likely to turn violent. He said she had stumbled on an invisible *duwende* that sat at the school gate admiring the girls as they walked in.

Five men came, and the healer then asked for a box of matches. It was given to him and he took a stick out of the box, muttered some secret words over it, and touched the middle toe on one of the girl's feet with the black tip of the matchstick.

In a man's voice the patient screamed in pain. "Don't! Oh, please don't!" she said. "It's painful!"

"Why did you get into this girl?" the healer demanded.

"Because she is sweet," came the male voice out of the girl's mouth. "I love her."

"Will you leave this girl or not?" demanded the healer.

No reply came, and the healer touched the patient's toe with the tip of the matchstick again.

In the man's voice the patient screamed in pain but made no reply. The patient turned violent and the five strong men had to hold her.

The healer touched her toe with the matchstick again and repeated his question.

"I will leave but would like to talk with Perlita first," the male voice replied out of the girl's mouth.

"Who is Perlita?" the healer asked.

The patient's mother replied that Perlita was the patient's best friend and classmate.

The patient's father went to ask Perlita to come over.

"Why?" Perlita asked.

"Your friend is possessed and he who has possessed her would like to talk to you," he replied. "Please come."

"I won't come," Perlita replied. "I'm scared."

The father went home and said Perlita refused to come. His wife then went to beg Perlita to come. Perlita put on a rosary around her neck and went with the patient's mother. Perlita sat down beside the patient's bed and asked what was troubling her.

"Please take off what's around your neck," said the patient in the old man's voice.

"What did you say?" Perlita asked.

"Take that thing off your neck," the voice repeated.

"I will not take it off unless you first leave my friend and promise never to return," Perlita said.

"I promise," said the voice. "Take it off."

Perlita took off the rosary and put it in her pocket. The patient's face then slowly relaxed and she was soon asleep, her body loose and her breathing easy.

She got up early next morning and asked, "Why do I feel so tired?"

That was the last time she and her family were bothered by a dwarf.

DWARFS ARE misshapen, stunted, ground-dwelling old men of legend. They are shown as owning stores of gold in European folklore. They live inside mountains, mounds, and mines. They are about the height of two-year-old children.

European dwarfs have kingdoms or tribes, kings, chiefs, and armies, and they reside underground in halls abounding in gold and precious stones. They are famed for their metal work and the magic swords they make. They are said to have great wisdom, expert knowledge, and the power to see the future. They are either invisible or can assume other forms to hide their identity.

In Norse mythology, dwarfs made Thor's powerful hammer and Odin's famous spear. Dwarfs guard hoarded gold in both the *Volsunga Saga* and the *Nibelungenlied*.

Dwarfs are shown to be generous and kind to friendly humans but revengeful when offended. The

Swiss dwarfs, called earth-men, often help farmers do their work, help them find their stray animals, and lead poor children to firewood or fruit they can gather. The dwarfs of Scandinavia and Germany sometimes steal corn, make livestock sickly or contrary, and, as with Philippine dwarfs, steal children and young girls. They repay service rendered to them by gifts of gold from their underground hoards. Those who steal dwarfs' gold or jewelry are punished with diseases. In the Philippines they find the gold to be nothing but cinders or ashes and the jewelry goat dung.

The fascination of people with the small size of dwarfs is shown by the fact that the early Egyptian pharaohs kept human dwarfs in their households.

Dwarfs played no role in Homeric and classical Greece, but in imperial Rome the children of slaves were sometimes stunted to increase their price.

The most common names of Philippine dwarfs are as follows:

ansisit—Iloko
calanget—Ifugao

caranget—Gaddang, Ibanag
duwende—various Hispanized groups
karanget—Ifugao
kutong-lupa—Tagalog
lakay—Iloko
lamang-lupa—Tagalog
lampong—Ilongot
matanda, matanda sa punso—Tagalog
muntianak—Bagobo
nuno, nuno sa punso—Hiligaynon, Tagalog
omayan—Manobo
sagay—Suringaonon
taong-lupa—Tagalog, "spirits of the fields or rice"—
various ethnolinguistic groups

It will be seen from the list that dwarfs are often
referred to by indirect names like "spirits of the fields,"
"lice of the earth," "old man," or "grandfather." These
names are used to avoid offending the creature by
directly naming it. Filipinos generally refer to snakes as
"the long ones" and rats as "the long-tailed ones" or
"the ladies" (*señoras*) so as not to offend them and thus
make them destructive. Fay Cooper-Cole, in his book
Peoples of Malaysia, reports that among the Semang
Negritos of Malaya, just across the South China Sea
from the Philippines, the names of animals are thought
to be so closely related to the animals named that to use
the real name of a fierce animal is likely to bring the
creature to whoever names it. "So," Cole wrote, "if you
are in the jungle you do not mention the tiger by name,
lest he come."

That Philippine dwarfs are invisible is indicated by
the following remark from Manuel and Lyd Arguilla's
Philippine Tales and Fables: "When passing near a mound
. . . stretch your hand before you saying, 'Old man of
the mound if it pleases you let me pass. . .' Being a
creature of the night he is not visible to mortal eyes."

Dwarfs are said to sometimes awaken friendly folk
at night to tell them to go and dig up a jar of gold but

must not be seen digging or bringing it out of the pit by anyone or the jar will sink out of sight, and its contents will turn to charcoal if it has been dug out.

Lucetta K. Ratcliff reports that a dwarf looked like a little old man to the farmer it appeared to. Emeterio C. Cruz learned from Alaska Filipinos that the *matanda sa punso* were "gray little old men." He added that as a group dwarfs were "pigmies with only one eye in the middle of the forehead and a huge nose with only one nostril."

The Iloko *ansisit* is said to be an old man as tall as a boy of three with large bodily joints, belly, head, eyes, nose, and mouth. He also dwells in caves and anthills. Like the European dwarf, he does not want the ground plowed by tractors since the weight of heavy machinery may make the roof of his home cave in.

A man once fired at a dwarf five times without hitting him.

The Ibanag *aran* is as short as a child two or three years old and has an old man's face and skin. His eyesight is poor since he wears no eyeglasses, but his hearing is excellent. He hears the conversation of people in kitchens under which he eavesdrops at dusk.

His hair is long and has a reddish tinge. His feet point the other way around so that he has gone south if his footprints point north and west if they point east. His toes are far apart since he has never worn shoes.

He courts pretty girls with sweet voices and beautiful names. He seduces girls to go with him into his underground realm where he has stores of gold and precious stones. Pretty girls wear necklaces of garlic or crocodile's teeth to keep him safely distant. Filipinos in the past had plain names since dwarfs were liable to seduce girls with nice-sounding names. Of late, however, Hollywood has reversed the old Filipino preference for plain old names in favor of glamorous names for children.

The word *duwende* is derived from the Spanish term for *dwarf*. It is today more commonly used than the old Philippine names for dwarfs.

A Hiligaynon dwarf is called *kama-kama*, and the
creature is a little man with short but muscular arms
and legs. His joints are large, and his fingernails are as
hard as chips from a carabao horn. He has a rough
brown skin, a round face, and high cheekbones. His
eyes are round, sharp, and dark, his mouth is large, and
his teeth are a dull brown in color. He has an old man's
high-pitched voice.

He lives deep in the ground which he enters and
leaves by passing through a termite mound on top of
which he often invisibly reclines or sits observing what
goes on. One should say "Excuse me, sir" when passing
by an anthill and add: "Please get out of the way since
I can't see you." One who fails to say that is liable to
step on him and then he will give him chills, fever, and
rashes.

The *calanget, kalango,* and *karanget* are believed in by
various Northern Luzon groups, these terms being
variants of what must have been the original name of
the dwarf in the region.

As the true owner of all the land there is, the dwarf
is paid rent by tillers of the soil.

The rent is in the form of boiled glutinous rice
without salt or spices. Dwarfs especially hate garlic,
ginger, and pepper.

Among the head-taking Ilongot of Northeastern
Luzon, the *lampong* is a dwarf said to shepherd wild
deer. A hunter once saw a lampong in the shape of
white deer with a single bright eye. He shot it with an
arrow five times without hitting it. His sixth shot
landed, and then the creature became a bright-eyed
two-foot dwarf with a long white beard.

The *aran* believed in by the Ibanag of the Cagayan
Valley is as short as a two- or three-years' child with an
old man's face and a wrinkled skin.

Tagalogs call the dwarf *matanda* (or *nuno*) *sa punso*
('old man' or 'grandfather of the termite mound'). He
has a long but sparse beard and a low nose. His ears
are large but not apical like those of some European

mythical beings. He wears a basket hat or a dried gourd helmet, and his shirt and pants are red or brown. He seduces pretty girls who have nice names and sweet voices. He takes them into his underground realm where he then makes them grow up and marries them.

A unique Philippine dwarf is the *tianak*, also known as *muntianak* among the Bagobos of Southeastern Mindanao and *patianak* among both the Tagalogs of Southern Luzon and the Mandayas of Eastern Mindanao. It has been described as the "spirit of a child whose mother died while pregnant, and who for this reason was born in the ground." In an otherwise fine monograph on the Southern Tagalogs, among whom he labored and was to be buried, Juan de Plasencia reported in 1589 that the patianak was a "woman and child who died in childbirth"— an obviously erroneous bit of etymologizing of *patianak* as *"patay na anak"* (dead child), since no mother and her child can become a single creature after they die. The belief Plasencia reported on occurs nowhere else as a spirit or otherwise in any folklore in the world.

The tianak is a demonological being instead of a human spirit or soul. It has been described as looking like "a naked newborn baby" and "a very plump baby lying on the side leaf of a banana plant." Two boys once came upon a tianak lying on a banana leaf in an isolated field at the end of the day. They thought it was a baby boy heartlessly left there by its mother. They picked it up and kissed it—whereupon it turned into a little old man with a wrinkled face and skin and a long beard, its nose flat, its eyes the size of *peseta* coins, and its right leg shorter than its left. It bit the arm of the boy carrying it, and he dropped it and the two boys ran away. The creature chased them by leaping on its longer leg.

The domicile of the Philippine dwarfs is usually underground, and they enter their realm through the narrow termite tunnels in mounds. They often invisibly rest on top of the mound. A dwarf seen in Alaminos, Laguna, however, is said to have lived in a long building under a large tree on the side of a hill. A man who had often been in the area but had never seen the building before now saw it. He entered and came to a long corridor with a room at one end. On each side of the corridor was a row of jars the contents of which he did not know since they were sealed. The European influence in this description is evident.

The Iloko *lakay* ('old man') and the Tagalog matanda sa punso ('old man of the mound') are both said to live in a termite mound, whence the creature's Tagalog name.

As in European folklore, the *sagay* dwarf believed in by Surigao folk is said to dwell in a gold mine, gold being plentiful in that area.

Godfrey Lambrecht wrote that the Gaddang of the upper Cagayan Valley call the dwarf *caranget* ('lice of the ground') and consider him the true owner of all the land. A farmer can till the land only as the creature's tenant, paying rent to him in the form of offerings before plowing the land and on the last day of harvest, in some cases when the rice blooms, too. This belief helps explain the widespread practice of placing offerings of unsweetened boiled glutinous rice, unsalted boiled white chicken that has gray or yellow leg scales, plus cigars and today even carbonated drinks, in the rice field before plowing and on the final day of harvest, and in some cases also when the rice starts to bloom. After serving their purpose as rent for the use of the land, these offerings are said to have virtue and are fed to children unless roaming dogs and pigs in the area first get to them.

Termite mounds are feared throughout the country, particularly mounds found under trees and in home lots. The folk are especially careful to avoid mounds with clean surroundings and on which no grass or weeds grow. Dwarfs are said to magically enter their underground realm through the narrow termite channels in these mounds. The Iloko are especially careful to say "Kayo-kayo!" (Away, away!) when compelled to go near or pass beside a termite mound.

The Iloko also say "Kayo-kayo" and the Tagalog

"Tabe po, nuno " ("Away, away" and "Away, grandfather") when throwing things in the yard or out of the window after dark for fear of hitting dwarfs that are said to be in the premises then. Nor should one sweep the yard or floor after sundown for fear of getting dust into the eyes of the dwarfs that are around human habitations at that hour.

Only when grass or shrubs are growing on a termite mound and dry leaves have settled on it do the folk consider it safe to walk close to or demolish it. Then they believe that the dwarf residing in the mound has left.

The rural Filipino's former preference for plain names for their children and for one another was a result of the belief in ground-dwelling dwarfs. Philippine folk say that dwarfs have poor eyesight but a sharp auditory sense, and they believe dwarfs enter house premises at sundown or shortly after, go under the eaves, and listen to the conversation upstairs. If a girl is called by a glamorous name or has a musical voice, the dwarfs in the premises will try to seduce her and take her into their underground realm. Till the influence of movies came and proved more powerful than the naming patterns imposed by this belief, Filipino children were called by such plain names ay Ayyang for Maria, Kulle for Juliana, Allong for Alejandro, and Okiong for Eulogio.

Girls cooking supper in the kitchen are warned to avoid singing or they will marry a widower or an old man. Such a groom is not human but a dwarf, and it is not called a dwarf for fear, as stated earlier, that to name a feared creature is to bring it close to one.

Possession by a demonological being is more commonly attributed to Philippine witches, but as in the legend, dwarfs are thought to possess people, too. The folk perhaps believe that if dwarfs can go in and out of their underground realm through the narrow passages in termite mounds, they should be able to get in and out of human bodies as well. Witches can also be made

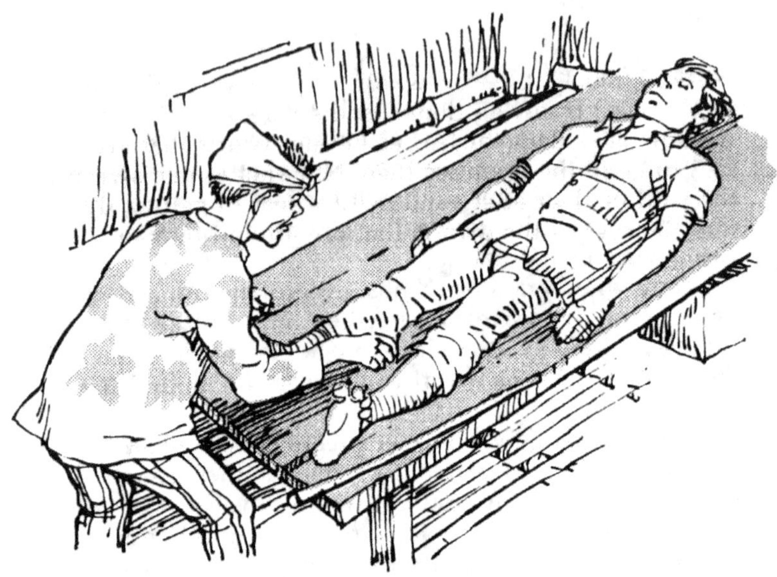

to reveal their possession of a patient by touching the
patient's toe with the tip of a matchstick as in the
legend. Why a matchstick is used indicates the antiquity
of the belief, antedating the production of fire by means
of matches instead of by striking a flint stone or by
cutting out a notch from a piece of dry bamboo which
one then wraps with dry moss or thin bamboo shavings
and vigorously rubbing that repeatedly on the cutting
edge of a bamboo splint anchored on the ground for
some ten minutes. When smoke appears on the moss or
shavings, one breathes into it and fire is soon produced.

The abundance of aromatic herbs grown around
rural Philippine homes is largely due to the belief that
these plants keep dwarfs away from the premises.
Citrus trees are generally planted around homes since
their sharp spines are thought effective in keeping
dwarfs and similar harmful environmental spirits away.
The crude cross set up and left standing for days on the
site where a house is to be built is intended to drive
away any dwarf residing in the spot. In the familiar
house-blessing ceremony, the priest mutters prayers

exorcising evil spirits while he sprinkles holy water in the hall, rooms, and premises. If one listens closely to the words he mutters, one will hear him exorcising hostile spirits which he may never have heard about but they are the demons, elves, dwarfs, and other environmental spirits, so called for lack of precise knowledge of them.

Unlike the bonnet-wearing European dwarfs, Philippine dwarfs wear basket hats or helmets from the shell of dried white squash fruit. They are barefoot, and their toes are far apart since they have never worn shoes. Floors are never swept at noon or after dark since dwarfs are said to be prying around in the premises then. Nor is water or rubbish thrown out of windows after sundown since dwarfs are thought to be in the yard at that time. One should say "Kayo-kayo!" (Away, away!) when throwing things in the yard at those hours because one is liable to hit a dwarf and the creature will inflict any of a wide variety of aches as a punishment or make the mouth of the guilty permanently awry, necessitating a folk cure.

The Elves

Letters from and to Frank

GLORIA and two other girls walked from their village to school in town through a small wood each morning and back again in the afternoon. Seventeen and high school seniors, they were all good-looking, but Gloria was the prettiest. She was graceful in her walk, and there was a pleasant tinkle in her voice.

It was their habit to stop under a *dalakit* tree to comb their hair and powder their noses before entering the town. One morning they found a fresh pink linen envelope on the smooth rock under the tree on which they placed their books and bags when they stopped. It was addressed to Gloria, and she tore it open, pulled out a matching pink sheet, and read:

> Dear Gloria,
>
> You are beautiful. Please be mine.
>
> Lovingly yours,
> Frank

The girls knew of no one named Frank and decided that it was just a joke. Gloria put the letter in her bag and the three hurried on to school.

During their library break, they decided to reply to the letter just to see what would happen. They wrote:

Dear Frank,

Do I know you?

Sincerely,
Gloria

They put the letter in an envelope and left it on the rock under the tree on their way home before sundown.

Another pink envelope addressed to Gloria was on the rock next morning. She picked it up, opened it, and read:

Dear Gloria,

I will be very happy to meet you. Just say where and when.

Forever yours,
Frank

The girl's next reply went:

Dear Frank,

At home. Whenever you wish.

Sincerely,
Gloria

They left the letter on the rock on their way home
as before. It was a Friday and Gloria sighed and said
that would be the last letter.

She was awakened by the voice of her brother at
midnight. "Gloria, Gloria," the voice said, "open the
door." He had gone serenading in the village with his
friends earlier in the evening and had now come
home—or so Gloria thought, lighting a small oil lamp
and opening the door.

In stepped a tall youth whom she had never seen
before. His complexion was fair, his nose long and thin,
his hair wavy and brown like corn tassels, and his eyes
blue like the sea. He was the best-looking man she had
ever seen outside the American movies in town.

"Who are you?" she asked.

"I'm Frank," he replied.

"What brings you here?"

"You wrote that I could come whenever I wished."

Then she gasped, for the next instant he had vanished without another word.

Gloria was found talking to herself in bed next
morning. Her parents did not send her to school on
Monday and sent for the herb healer instead. He came,
looked her over, shook his head, and said, "This girl
has a *dalakitnon* lover."

Gloria's two friends were remorseful because what
they had thought a harmless prank had disordered their
poor friend's mind. They mentioned the letters, and the
healer nodded his head and said: "She wrote the
dalakitnon that he could visit her. He did, and now she
is in his power."

Gloria was dead in half a year, and the people knew
that her dalakitnon lover had taken her to his world in
the dark woods.

IN THE LANGUANGE of folklore, elves differ from
fairies in that they are loners, while fairies have social
organizations. Elves may have families but have none of
the larger social groups that the European fairies have.

There are fairy courts, dances, and social ranks, but
elves live as isolates or in groups no larger than nuclear
families.

The fairies are forest dwellers like the elves, too, but
they have kings, queens, princess and princesses, and
nobles and their ladies and serving men and women.
There are no such ranks and social organizations among
elves.

In a country with some eighty native languages—by
which no intercommunication is possible or they would
be just dialects—the elves are known by a wide variety
of names. These include:

aghoy — Waray
dalakitnon — Waray
dayamdam — Agusanon
engkantada, engkanto — Bikol, Sugbuhanon, and other
    Hispanized groups
kamanan-daplak — Zambali
kiba-an — Iloko
palasekan — Ilongot
ragit-ragit — Romblomanon
tamawo — Hiligaynon
tirtiris — Iloko
wenri-wenri — Romblomanon

Rural Filipinos seem oblivious of who own the fruit
trees they raid by the wayside. They just pick the fruit
of trees they pass by without asking permission from
the owner. But they are most careful to beg the elves
thought to reside in the trees to let them do so. Before
he cuts down a tree, the Ilokano says:

Bari-bari;
Dikay agungunget, pari,
Ta adda papukan diay padi.
(Your excuse, please:
Be not angry, friends,
For the priest asked us to fell something.)

Villagers are careful not to throw things in their
yards, particularly after sunset when elves are said to be

there, without saying:

    Kayo-kayo! (Away, away!)

Elves whose premises are trespassed are said to throw dust into the trespassers' eyes and to give them skin rashes and permanently twisted lips. The folk healer cures these afflictions by casting rice on the premises violated and expressing regret for the trespass.

Some children are said to lose their hair to the foot-tall female *kiba-an,* which steals the hair to keep hers long enough to reach her feet that point in the wrong direction. Further theft of the hair is prevented by crushing flies on the bald scalp and rubbing them on.

The kiba-an is also blamed for coconuts having too little water and meat, and the creature can be driven off by smudging the trees with burning bovine hooves. It steals greens from gardens and, cornered, turns itself into a paling in the fence which screams in pain when the gardener sweeps the fence with a stick. The kiba-an are also kept away from fish traps in streams by displaying small bamboo crosses on the traps. No such crosses are needed for traps set in tidal waters since

demonological beings, except the merfolk and dragons,
are said to fear salt water.

The favorite domiciles of elves and their neighbors—
namely the demons such as the kapre—are the
kalumpang and the *dalakit*. These trees have thick leaves
and their branches gracefully arch down and they often
dominate the landscape. Termite mounds develop under
them, and since these mounds are thought to be the
gateway of dwarfs into their underground realm, the
folk keep away from them.

Elves are said to climb into trees by way of the
bagbagutot, a shrub with tiny edible black berries. It
clambers up the trunks of trees in thickets.

A large kalumpang tree stands across the street from
the Chemistry department of the University of the
Philippines, in Diliman, and the stink from its fly-
pollinated blooms compete with that from the nearby
laboratories. An even larger such tree stands beside the
Marikina Road across from St. Joseph's Church in
Quezon City. Another large such tree stood on top of
the seventeenth-century wall of Intramuros, in Manila,

right next to the *Manila Bulletin* building until it was felled by some brave souls recently.

The tree from which the dalakitnon ('one who lives in the dalakit tree') got its name is the dalakit. It starts as a seed dropped by a bird or bat in the crotch of a tree in the moist jungle, germinates there, and slowly sends roots around the trunk of its host and on down into the ground. As the seedling grows, its roots enlarge and tighten their hold around the host tree. They go on multiplying and enlarging till the trunk of the host withers and leaves a hollow where bats, owls, snakes, monitor lizards, and geckos den. The tree sends down adventitious roots from its low-hanging branches as well. The tree and the sounds made by the creatures denning in it inspire awe and fear in the beholder.

Gilda Cordero-Fernando, fictionist and publisher of coffee-table books, has a large dalakit growing in her front yard in Quezon City. This impressive-looking tree is a centerpiece in the yards of same large residential homes in Manila's suburbs.

Elves and the Philippine version of the Arabian genie, locally known as the kapre, are said to live in various large trees but especially prefer the *Sterculia foetida*, known to Ilokanos as bangar, to Tagalogs as kalumpang, and to Visayans as bubog. It is a handsome tree, its palmate leaves thick and its branches arching down. It is not suitable as an ornamental tree, however, because it bears tiny inconspicuous blooms that smell like feces and are pollinated by flies and for this reason are called takang demonio ('demon's excrement') by the Mt. Pinatubo Negritos in Zambales.

Some elves are just a few inches tall and others about a foot, but the rest are six-footers or taller. The tall elves include the dalakitnon of the legend about Gloria. They freely interact with humans, going to public dances, driving flashy new cars, and winning beauty contests. Some of them even go on fellowships in Europe and North America. But they all live in trees in the Philippines. People imagine that the dalakit and

kalumpang are trees but these are elf mansions and some
have heard the clink of elf plates in elf kitchens and
dining tables in these trees.

A pretty college girl from the city once went with
her classmate to the latter's quiet frontier village to
spend her summer vacation there. She met a tall, blond
youth at a village dance given in her honor. They
danced and danced and then she agreed to go with him
and visit his folks that same night. In his gleaming
sports car they drove to a wondrous city with bright
lights, wide streets, and splendid homes. She was found
weeping alone in the deep woods next day after a long
and anxious search by the village folk.

The lack of social organizations among these early
Philippine deities helps explain the Filipino's inability to
form and maintain his. Filipino clubs overseas quickly
break up into warring splinter groups, usually along
linguistic and regional lines, and this in spite of 500
years of Filipino apprenticeship in social living under
the Spaniards and Americans.

The special attraction of the dalakitnon to Gloria
was that he had the physical traits of the conquering
Spanish and American Caucasoid—tall, light-complexioned, blond, his nose long and narrow, and his eyes
blue rather than dark brown or black like a Filipino's.
The elves in some Philippine legends also have no
philtrum—the depression on the upper lip beneath the
nose. The Visayan *engkanto* has such a transparent
throat that water can be seen going down his pharynx
when he drinks. The kiba-an have gold teeth and grin
to light their path on dark nights.

Over the centuries Philippine girls have preferred
whites to blacks or browns as dating partners and
spouses. During the Spanish conquest the native males
often complained that the girls were always leaving
them to join white Spaniards. This writer was at the
beach in Southern Zambales before daybreak on January
30, 1944, when an American invasion force landed to
cut off the fierce Japanese defenders of Lingayen Beach

up North. He then saw many Filipino girls running out to offer green coconuts to the white Americans, some even holding hands with them. But the same girls fled in panic when the black contingents, landing separately, came ashore.

Mangyans with Caucasoid features were reported in the 1960s to be living in an isolated community in Mindoro Island. They were said to be descendants of seventeenth-century Dutch sailors whose warship capsized off the coast of the island. This is possible because the Spaniards fought off several Dutch naval invasions near the mouth of Manila Bay in the seventeenth century.

The number of white men's offspring around Philippine military bases occupied by Americans is far larger than the black men's children though there have not been many more whites than blacks at these bases.

In 1974 this writer saw a barefoot road worker with a white man's features on the construction site of the Pan-Philippine Highway in Samar during a trip through the area. He and the children of white American and brown Filipino liaisons of today and the recent past will be among the elves in tomorrow's legends. Whites have also increased in numbers with the coming of multinationals in banana and pineapple plantations in Mindanao, and the presence of mining prospectors, crocodile and orchid hunters, scuba divers, and tourists and businessmen. In short, accounts like these were evidently invented by Filipinos eager to keep their dating partners and spouses.

A legend of the vanishing hitchhiker, common in the West, is told by a parish priest from Lobo, Batangas. He was driving his Volkswagen one night when he heard the door open and close with a bang. He switched on the light in the car and saw an attractive woman in a red dress in the back seat. He drove faster because of fear. Then he heard the door close with a bang and found her gone when he looked.

A similar legend is told by another Batangas priest.

He was on the last bus from Manila and a woman in red beside him asked for a cigarette. He gave it to her and she smoked it and then asked for another. He gave that to her, too. He then got off at a corner with some of his parishioners at 10:00 P.M. and asked them if they knew the woman. They replied that they never saw her.

In some legends, elves offer unpolished rice, called "engkanto rice" in Quezon Province, to their intended captives. It is said that if one eats the rice, it turns into worms in his mouth and he remains in the elves' power. This belief helps explain why rural Filipinos refuse to eat unpolished rice no matter how often they are told that higly polished rice does not contain the anti-beriberi Vitamin B_1 found on the seed coat of un-polished rice.

The Iloko word *naugaw* describes a person wasteful of rice. It is derived from *ugaw*, an elf. The folk level the rice in a bin and place an inverted coconut-shell bowl on it to keep elves away. A string of empty snails is also laced around the neck of a jar used as a rice bin to keep elves away by the tinkle of the shells when these creatures clamber up the sides of the bin.

It may be that because this writer often heard it as a youngster, his favorite folktale is one his mother often told at bedtime. She was a fine raconteur and a good reader but had not been taught how to write for fear that like Gloria in the legend, she might write letters to suitors not on the approved list. Her tale was about Juan and the bangar tree, and it went this way:

Juan's widowed mother kept begging him to go to the forest and get some firewood because her woodbox was empty. He kept saying he would go but never did. But one morning when she began weeping, he put his axe on his shoulder, walked into the forest, stopped at the foot of a bangar tree, and playfully said: "I will cut you down, bangar,/ To be my mother's mortar."

A kiba-an came down from the tree and said, "Spare this tree, Juan, for my wife has just given birth." The kiba-an then produced a small clay pot and added, "For your kindness, I will give you this pot. You need only hold it up and say 'Rice still hot/ And pork in my pot' and it will give you all the food you can eat."

Juan took the pot and left.

Night fell on his way home and he stopped in a hut by the road. He begged for shelter and the widow housekeeper let him in. He took out his magic pot, said 'Rice still hot/And pork in my pot," and they feasted on steaming rice and sizzling pork.

The widow woke him up early at dawn, gave him a pot that looked just like Juan's pot, and he left.

Juan's mother was displeased to see that he had brought no firewood home. He said she had no need for firewood, took out the pot, and said, "Rice still hot/ And pork in my pot."

Neither rice nor pork appeared in the pot and he smashed it, picked up his axe, soon stood at the foot of the bangar tree, and said, "I will cut you down, bangar,/To be my mother's mortar."

Down came the father kiba-an holding a small
purse. He shook the purse and bright pieces of gold fell
at Juan's feet. He begged Juan to spare the tree, and
Juan took the purse, shouldered his axe, and left.

He dropped in at the old widow's hut by the road
at nightfall, asked her to spread a mat, shook the purse
over it, and out dropped bright pieces of gold. She went
to buy cooked food at the market and they feasted and
then he went to bed.

She woke him up early, gave him a purse that
looked just like his purse, and wished him a pleasant
journey home.

Juan's mother was displeased to see that he had
brought home no firewood. He told her to spread a
mat, she did, and he shook the purse over it. Nothing
dropped out, and she begged him to go and get her
some firewood at last.

Juan hurried back to the woods and was just about
to start whacking at the bangar tree when the kiba-an
came down holding a rope, a whip, and a drum. He
told the drum to beat, and it beat out a rhythm so
urgent that Juan took it, the rope, and the whip and
went on his way home.

He told the old widow in the hut by the road to
prepare to hear wonderful music when he got to her
hut. Then he told the drum to play, and it beat out a
rhythm so compelling that she began dancing, but the
rope tied her up and the whip beat her until she
begged Juan to stop the drum and she would give him
back his pot and his purse.

Juan did so, and never again had his mother any
occasion to mention firewood.

The Ghouls

The Tuba Gatherer and the Corpse Thief

A MAN CLIMBED to the top of a tall coconut tree in a grove at sunset. Into a bamboo tube hitched to his shoulder by means of a crook he poured out the pink liquor that had dripped into another bamboo tube into which he had inserted the ends of racemes of coconut blooms he had clipped anew the morning before.

He glanced at his house below as he did this and saw a man go up the bamboo ladder, push the door open, and get in. The stranger then came out onto the *batalan*—the open back porch where the household washing and drying was done—bearing something heavy on his shoulder, walked down the ladder, and headed toward a banana grove.

The wine gatherer suddenly realized that what the man had borne on his shoulder was his wife. She had been ailing for almost a month and was in bed when he left to gather the coconut-bloom sap.

He hurried down the trunk of the coconut tree and sprinted toward his house. In the bed he found a corpse that looked just like his wife in both physical features and in her sleeping gown. He remembered what certain harmful creatures of legend were said to sometimes do to the dying or the dead. He quickly opened the hand of the corpse and looked at the balls of its fingertips. He found them to be just plain skin with none of the whorls of fine lines characteristic of human fingertips.

Quickly he heaved the corpse to his shoulder, staggered to the window, and dropped it to the ground. Then to he rushed down to look.

Only the trunk of a banana tree from which the leaves had been lopped off lay where what appeared to be his wife had dropped.

With his bolo he hurried to the bamboo fence
around his coconut grove and pulled out a slender
stake. He sharpened the top of the stake and then
dashed with it to the banana grove. He looked around
in the darkened grove and could see nothing there. But
when he looked under a thick clump of banana trees,
he saw the man bent over his pale wife and attempting
to disrobe her while she tried to brush his hands off.
He recognized the man as one whom his neighbors had
called an aswang, and indeed he looked fiercer than he
had ever looked before as he went around in the village.

The wine gatherer unsheathed his bolo, raised it,
and told the creature to keep off his wife. The creature
snarled at him and continued trying to disrobe her.
Then the wine gatherer set upon him with his bolo. He
tried to stab him, but the blade harmlessly slipped off
the creature's body every time.

Finally the wine gatherer sheathed his bolo, picked
up the bamboo spear he had brought, and pressed its
sharp point to the creature's upper back.

Only then did the creature let go of the man's wife.
He rose, slipped through the banana grove, and was
lost among the close-set trunks and long dry leaves that
hung limply, draping them.

The man's wife made a moan, and he sighed with
relief to find her alive.

He gently gathered her in his arms and bore her
home. He sponged her with water boiled with aromatic
herbs and fed her with soft rice spiced with lemon
grass.

She was up and about in a few days, and never
again was the weredog seen in the neighborhood.

THE DEMONOLOGICAL being that figures in the
above legend is the first of five types of legendary
creatures known as aswang in various areas of the
Philippines: (1) the corpse-eater or ghoul, (2) the blood
sucker or vampire, (3) the self-segmenter or viscera

sucker or viscera-taker, (4) the werebeast (*werewolf* in
European folklore, but that term is inapplicable in the
Philippines where there are no wolves, and besides, the
variety of the creature found in the Philippines is said
to be capable of assuming different animal shapes such
as hogs, goats, and carabaos as well as dogs), and (5)
the hexer or witch.

The ghouls of Philippine folklore are commonly
known in the archipelago by these local names:

aswang as a corpse-eater—various ethno-linguistic
    groups
balbal—Tagbanua
calag—Hiligaynon
damdam—Tagbanua
ebwa —Tinguian
segben—various Visayan groups
wir-wir—Apayao

Since werebeasts are said to steal and then devour
the dead, and since death is the most gripping event in
human passage, the beliefs about ghouls have played a
most important role in shaping Philippine culture. Even
in those areas of the country where the creature is no
longer known by name and no legends are told about
it, such as in Southern Zambales where this writer was
born, grew up, and recently returned to live for a dozen
years, certain customs related to death and the dying
are otherwise inexplicable except that they were shaped
by the folks' fear of ghouls. Anthropologist F. Landa
Jocano writes in the introduction to his *The Philippines
at the Spanish Contact* (1975):

> Culturally, another cause of residential mobility
> among pre-Hispanic as well as contemporary upland
> Filipinos was the belief in the active participation of
> the spirits in the lives of men. Should any member
> of the family become seriously ill or die, the people
> believed that the spirits of the fields had been of-
> fended and therefore the residents should move out.
> The dwellings were either left behind or burnt

before departure. When seen in terms of this cultural millieu, laboring hard in building stone dwellings or buildings that might have to be burned afterward would be impractical. Nor would it be logical for the community to build megalithic structures only to leave these for another place. Because of these social and cultural factors, reinforced by the nature of agricultural pursuits, it is in fact doubtful whether it is valid to speak of "temples" or to accept the term to apply to pre-Hispanic "places of adoration," as most [Spanish] chronicles did.

Writing in 1838-1839 about the mortuary customs of the West Visayans, Jose Maria y Pavon noted:

The first thing which they did on the death of their ancestors was to perform the *larao* (which signifies the mourning). This consisted in not eating anything for many days and, at the end, for three consecutive days. During these days, however, they indulged much in intoxication. At night they watched, for it was said that if they did not do so, the aswang would come and eat the liver if the diseased were young, and if he were old, the guts. ... During those night watches, there was usually much noise and shouting, for since this was pleasing and exciting to them, they thus forgot, it was said, their sad memories, and in this way, they made the death house a place of merriment.

Pavon clearly misread, however, the noise and shouting at those Philippine wakes. It was not to make the mourners forget their sad memories and make the bereaved house a place of merriment. The singing and noise at Philippine wakes, still much in evidence today at funeral parlors even in the large cities, was not to make the bereaved forget their memories and the house where a death has just occurred a place of merriment. Grief is too deep-seated to be thus dispelled. It was meant to keep ghouls at a safe distance since these corpse-eaters were then as now believed to crowd around homes where the dead lay in state before burial. A.R. Radcliffe Brown, a more perceptive contemporary anthropologist, wrote on a similar custom of the Andaman Islanders, in the Indian Ocean just west of the Philippines:

> The burial . . . is conducted, if possible, on the day of death. If it has to be deferred till the morrow all the inhabitants of the camp keep awake. The relatives sit round the corpse weeping at intervals, while some of the men take it in turns to sing songs during the hours of darkness. This, so they say, is to keep away the spirits that have caused the death, and so prevent them from further mischief. When a man or woman dies in the prime of life after a short illness, the friends and relatives often break out in anger which they express in different ways. A man will shout threats and curses at the spirits that he conceives to be responsible for the death of his friend. He may pick up his bow and arrow and discharge the arrows in all directions or in some other way give expression to his angry feelings.

The Philippine ghouls are reported to steal human corpses and then devour them. Their breath is said to have a sickening smell because they eat decaying flesh, and they have curved, hard nails and sharp teeth for tearing up flesh.

Ghouls are said to be generally invisible, but they reportedly look just like ordinary folk when seen. They reside in or near human habitations. They congregate in flocks in trees close to burial grounds at night, descend on fresh graves, and dig the corpses out. This belief may have led to the popularity of concrete tombs as soon as cement became available in the country. The dead were formerly buried directly in the ground, and even today the afterbirth is placed in a small clay pot and buried under the fireplace.

Ghouls are said to transform the corpse into the body of a pig and in its place put a banana trunk which they have first made to look exactly like the dead except that the balls of its fingertips do not have the fine lines in whorls used in modern fingerprinting for crime detection. They then devour the corpse at leisure and try to feed their neighbors with parts of it to make them ghouls like themselves since ghouls prefer to flock together and attack in large numbers.

The auditory sense of ghouls has often been remarked on. They can hear the sounds attendant to death over great distances. This helps explain the widespread practice of repeatedly shouting the names of the Christian trinity beside a dying person and the attempts to avoid wailing over the dead in bereaved Philippine homes. It is reported that ghouls use the mouths of mortars to monitor the sounds attendant to death and are then guided by these sounds to find the dying or the dead.

Ghouls are said to know that a patient is near death when he smells like ripe jackfruit (*Artocarpus hetero-*

phylla Lmk.) To sample a patient's scent, they go under
the house where the sick lies, hoist themselves up on a
floor joist beneath his bed, and inhale deep. If the
patient smells right, they stick around.

Ghouls communicate the precise location of the dead
or dying to one another and then congregate there.
They devour corpses right at the grounds or carry them
up into the nearby trees and feast on them there. Their
appetite whetted by the flavor of dead flesh, they are
said to cause the death of and devour the surviving
relatives of the departed as well. This belief helps
explain why in many areas in the country, the house
where there has been a death is burned down and the
location abandoned, thus worsening the country's
deforestation problems because of swidden tillage.
Death may indeed often occur in the same household,
but this is caused by infection, though the unschooled
survivors of the dead have never heard of the germ
theory of disease and can blame only the legendary
causes of death which they inherited from their fore-
bears, and indeed their notion is more dramatic than
the idea that a disease is caused by minute bacteria.

Ghouls are reportedly warded off by fire, metals, and spices. They are also reported to be kept off by loud speech and vociferous singing and games and by the presence of numerous guests at vigils. Miguel de Loarca, a Spanish colonizer, in a book published in Arevalo, Iloilo, in 1582, reported that the Filipinos kept a fire burning under the house where the dead lay in state to make the ghouls keep away.

The illumination is excessive around the coffin not only in Philippine villages but especially in urban funeral parlors where electricity is available. This phenomenon is a carry over from the days when fires were kept burning under and around the house where the dead lay in state. In many areas the orphans wear red strips of cloth on their clothes. This is meant to protect them, for ghouls fear fire and red is the color of fire.

A bolo is placed beside the corpse lying in state, for ghouls are said to fear bladed weapons—a belief that lends support to the theory that demonological beings such as ghouls entered the human belief system before iron came into use.

Since sweeping might scatter the dust containing the smell of the dead and bring the ghouls over, the floor of the house where there is a dead is not swept till three days after the burial. The next of kin go to the river for a communal bath, washing their hair with water poured through the ashes of burned rice straw three days after the burial. Into the river they also cast off the clothes in which the patient died.

The neck of a chicken is slashed and the fowl thrown from the top of the ladder and allowed to flutter away and die just before the coffin is borne away for burial. This is intended to attract the ghouls that are in the premises of the bereaved house from the dead to the bleeding fowl.

In the West, the dead lies in state in a closed coffin and is lowered into the grave unseen. But Philippine coffins are provided with a transparent glass window above the face of the dead, and the lid is kept open while the dead lies in state at home or in a funeral parlor. The mourners and visitors keep their eyes on the face of the dead while they grieve. This is because of the belief, illustrated by the legend this chapter starts with, that ghouls are said to replace the dead or the dying with a look-alike banana trunk and then carry off the corpse. Several natives from rural Iloilo have confirmed that this belief is still common in their area of the country. A civilian employee at the U.S. Communications Base at San Miguel, Zambales, told this writer that back in his native Iloilo he had dropped out of his window what appeared to be the body of a dead relative and found it transformed into a banana trunk when he went down to check under the window.

The custom of inserting bladed tools between the slats in the bamboo floor of the typical rural Philippine house and the practice of bathing the convalescent and washing the newly dead with decoctions from plants with a strong aroma such as the a*lagao* of the Iloko and Tagalog, the *baraniw* of the Iloko and *tanglad* of the Tagalog—popularly known as lemon grass—the leaves of the guava (*Psidium guajava* L.), the juice of the *kala-mansi* (*Citrus microcarpa* Bunge), and the *sambong* (Tagalog) or *subusob* (Iloko), known to botanists as *Blumea balsamefera* — all are survivals from the ancient belief in ghouls that could be kept at a safe distance by the use of these plants.

The noise at Filipino gatherings can be seen as a social pattern born of the belief that there are ghouls. An American researcher found that the radios loaned to the Philippine barrios to bring socially useful information to isolated villages were used to create noise at public gatherings rather than to transmit information. Filipinos debate in verse at vigils for the dead. In Central and Northern Luzon, guests are fed for days while the dead lies in state. Luz B. Amparo, the school principal at Lobo, Batangas, reported that Geraldine Malatico, and A.B. in Political Science from the University of

Washington who was a Peace Corps Volunteer in Lobo in 1966-1968, wondered why the local schoolchildren were so noisy when in groups. Any Filipino reader will perhaps recall the schoolchildren's noise before the bell and at recess as his most distinct impression of his first days in school.

Many Filipinos refuse to go to bed though seriously ill. They say they will grow worse if they lie down and are most eager to get out of bed before they fully recover. Our medical doctors gripe that too many patients do not see them before they are past cure.

Also as a consequence of the belief in ghouls, extra beds are provided for close relatives to sleep in during the night in Philippine hospital rooms—a phenomenon unknown in the West. This was probably born of the belief that ghouls are in constant reconnaissance for the ailing and the dead to attack and are invisibly perched in the trees in hospital grounds planted there to keep the area nice and cool.

Schoolteachers complain that their students seldom admit they are ill till they are past cure. The youngsters fear that to admit that they are sick is to admit that they have violated their elders' ban on trespassing in thickets, groves, and deserted areas feared as the domain of disease-causing demonological beings.

Sol Torrijos, a pharmacist, reports that ghouls reportedly gain admission into hospital wards as patients and then prowl in the wards at night.

In many a Visayan village, the family members lie down to sleep on the family mat so positioned that no two adjacent sleepers' heads point in the same direction. This is to give optimum mutual protection to the sleepers, for it results in an equal distribution of the sleepers' lines of sight in relation to the windows. This also explains why only two sides of the typical village house has windows, the walls under the two gables being windowless.

To the belief in ghouls can also be traced the large size as well as the noise of Filipino families, for the more noisy the members, the safer life for every member is thought to be. It is easy to spot Filipinos on international plane flights—and Filipinos like to travel

in tightly knit groups. The noisiest group in such gatherings are almost certain to be Filipinos on their way to
an international gathering.

Philippine wakes for the dead feature noisy parlor
games and songs that last till daybreak. At a recent
wake for the dead, the folk who had played cards
around tables finally declared that it was morning and
time to disperse. One of them looked out of the window and said, "Yes, they have left." He meant the
ghouls that had invisibly hovered around the house all
night tying to get in and steal the dead.

The Philippines is perhaps the only country with a
law against blaring radios on passenger buses—a law
which, however, continues to be ignored by bus drivers
and tolerated by passengers who believe that the noise
keeps ghouls safely distant.

The Giants

Angngalo and Aran

THERE WAS THE SKY above but no sea below when the world was new. There was only land below, and it stretched far and wide without mountains, hills, rivers, and valleys. Not a single man, woman, or child lived in the whole wide world.

Two giants, Angngalo and Aran, his wife, lived at the beginning of the world. They were so tall that they could touch the sky when they reached up, and so long were their legs that at a single stride they could go from the Ilocos country up in the north of Luzon to what is today the Manila area in the Tagalog country in the south. No mention is made in this myth of the Bikol region, the Visayan Islands, Palawan, and Mindanao. This may be taken to mean that these regions were an altogether different world in those earliest times since Angngalo and Aran could have reached them all by just taking a short step or two.

An unnamed god asked Angngalo to create mountains and seas. With his hands Angngalo scooped earth from the ground and put it in piles, and these became what we now know as mountains and hills. In time grass, herbs, shrubs, and trees grew on the mountains and hills and in the valleys and plains, too. Insects and birds and then larger animals appeared, and the world was soon full of living things.

Then Angngalo spat on the ground, and from his spit the first man and the first woman were born. Angngalo called the first man Lalake and the first woman Babae, and today a man is still called *lalake* and a woman *babae* everywhere in the country.

One day Angngalo passed water into the holes in the ground he had scooped earth out of. The water became lakes, rivers, and seas. Fish and sea animals appeared. These multiplied, and their descendants are the sea animals and fish of today.

One day Angngalo put Lalake and Babae in a piece of bamboo known as *buho* or *bulo* today and let it float on the sea. Lalake and Babae got out of the piece of bamboo and built their home, and they became the first Filipinos.

Angngalo saw that Lalake and Babae were unhappy. Their surroundings were drab, he realized, and were without color. So he made the sun, the moon, and the stars and hung them up in the sky above. Lalake and Babae admired the beauty of these heavenly bodies in the blue sky above and were happy.

In time three pretty but gigantic daughters were born to Angngalo and Aran. The girls grew up and became beautiful young women. They complained that the sea was not salt enough. One day Angngalo decided

to take salt in bags to the Manila area in the Tagalog
county to the south. He made a large boat and loaded it
with salt in bags. The girls boarded the boat with him
and on the way playfully dropped some of the salt into
the sea. The salt melted, and the sea became salt.

Back home in the Ilocos land, Angngalo's three
daughters went to bathe in the sea one morning. They
walked into the water and shouted with glee. Then the
wind blew from across the sea and the wind rose. "Save
us, Father!" they shouted to Angngalo. "We are drowning!"

Angngalo rushed down to the sea, stood waist-deep
in the water, and let his loin cloth —his *baag* — soak in
the water. The sea went down and the girls were saved
from drowning. Then Angngalo squeezed his loin cloth
dry, and the sea rose and grew as deep as it had been
before.

THE FOREGOING legend is here retold from a report
by Alfredo B. Villanueva in E. Arsenio Manuel's folklore
collection.

Giants are large hominoids of mythology which, unlike the similarly large creatures of folklore—the ogres—are typically not man eaters. Giants live farther as a rule from human communities than do the ogres, many of whom reside close to clearings and even in human villages to be close to their prey. The giants of Greek and Scandinavian mythology existed before and were overcome in battle by the higher gods.

The giants of European folklore are often cruel but feeble-minded. The folk and even small animals easily overcome them by use of their wit. Some marriages occur between humans and giants' daughters—never giants' sons—but the folk generally avoid giants. This suggests that giant tales and legends may in part have developed out of traditions of early races living close to more advanced groups who had taken over the land but failed to eliminate the earlier settlers.

All Philippine giants have human shape except the *bannog* of Northern Luzon which was an enormous bird, and the *ikugan* of Southern Mindanao, a powerful large monkey.

The names of most Philippine giants are capitalized and in Roman type in printed accounts of them to show their close affinity with humans. These names include the following:

Angngalo—Iloko
Aran—Iloko
Ararayat—Zambale
bannog — Iloko, Tinguian
Bekat—Isneg
Bungisngis—Tagalog
Buringcantada—Bicol
Gawigawen—Tinguian
Gisurab, Gisarub—Apayao, Isneg
Gungay—Apayao
ikugan—Manobo
Kalapaw—Isneg
Sappaw—Apayaw
Sibbarayungan, Sibbarayonna—Apayao, Isneg
Sumarang—Iloko
Surab—Apayao

The giants told about in world folklore may have the shapes of birds and beasts as well as humans.

The giants of Greek mythology were known as *titans*. They were enormous hominoids that populated the world at the beginning of time. The Scandinavian giants were similarly huge beings antedating and overcome by the later deities led by Odin. The giants in folk traditions around the world were generally human in form but were of an enormous size and were slain in battle by much smaller gods that came into the world after them. In his *Paradise Lost*, John Milton, who had done extensive research in Hebrew as well as Greco-Roman mythology before he sat down to compose his masterpiece blind by dictating an average of seventy lines which he had composed and memorized the night before, indicated the enormous size of the Hebraic angels, describing one of them as casting a shadow over a vast area in the North African desert.

Later Philippine giants were relatively smaller than Angngalo and Aran. Only Ararayat seems to have approximated their great size. The Zambale say that a lake just outside Candelaria, in Northern Zambales, resulted when Ararayat scooped up earth from the land and piled it in the Central Luzon Plain. This became today's Mount Arayat in Pampanga. Large depressions in the shape of human footprints said to be those of Ararayat are reported to exist near the hill village of Poonbato, just east of Botolan, Zambales—a belief with many analogues around the world.

Most Philippine giants have human shapes. But the bannog of Northern Luzon was a bird large enough to carry a carabao to its nest in a treetop on a high cliff. The ikugan of Southeastern Mindanao was a powerful large monkey with a murderous tail. A bannog swooped down from the sky in a Tinguian tale and seized a hunter in its talons. It then flew off with him to its eyrie at the top of a large tree in the mountains and left him there to feed its chicks with. He waited for the chicks to put on wings, eating of the meat their mother periodically brought in to feed them. When the fledglings left the nest, he held on to the leg of one of them and let go when it fluttered close to the ground.

Another bannog in an Iloko tale obscured the sky as it flew down and one after another carried into the air a carabao, a horse, a monkey, and a pig assigned to stay and watch the basket of fish which the animals had caught in the sea. The smallest of the fishers, a tortoise, then tricked the bannog into digging a large pit in the sand to hide in and into positioning a large rock at the mouth of the pit. The bannog jumped in to hide in alarm after the tortoise said the world was just about to end, and the tortoise pushed the rock and crushed the bannog in the pit.

Bungisngis is described in a Tagalog tale as a giant fond of grinning, his name being derived from the Tagalog word *ngisi*, 'to grin'. His upper lip is said to be so wide that when he grins it curls back and covers his face and then one can run away. He once seized a carabao by the horns and threw it knee-deep into the ground.

Buringcantada, a Bikol giant, had but one eye—on his forehead. His incisors were long tusks projecting from the corners of his mouth.

In one of his series of readings published by Ginn and Co., of Boston, the only prescribed reading material in all Philippine grade schools during the American regime, Camilo Osias wrote about several boys who entered a large house belonging to a giant. They saw the giant coming and climbed into the ceiling. The giant entered, heard them there, and asked who they were. They replied that they were giants. Then he asked them to prove their great size, and to the floor they dropped a piece of rope they had picked up on the road and said that this was a strand of their hair. The giant then asked them to drop one of their teeth, and they dropped an axe head. The giant finally asked them to speak, and the boys beat on a big bass drum and the giant panicked, ran away, and never came back.

Gawigawen was a six-headed giant among the Tinguians, whom anthropologist Fay Cooper-Cole, author of a monograph on them, identified in a public lecture at Indiana University in 1948 as the probable ancestors of the Iloko. Gawigawen's great size and strength are indicated by the remark in a tale that his spear and head axe were "as big as the sky."

Guisurab was a ferocious Isneg giant who killed everyone in a human village. Gisarub was a large cannibal giant among the Apayao.

The *ikugan*, which the Manobo of Mindanao tell about, was a ferocious simian giant, its name meaning 'tailed'. With its powerful tail it reached out to the rear of its enemy and then overpowered him by attacking him from in front.

The Isnegs tell about the giant Kalapaw, human in shape but able to tear down large coconut trees with his strong arms. He was so large that he walked past the province of Apayao at a single stride. The Apayao also tell about the giant Sappaw whose name suggests its likely identity with Kalapaw, the giant whom the Isnegs tell about. Sappaw had human neighbors whose daughters he could not wed since they were too small for him.

Pedro Bukaneg's Iloko poem—some call it an epic— *Biag ni Lam-ang* (Life of Lam-ang) tells about the narrative hero Lam-ang encountering Sumarang, a giant, on his way to visit the beautiful but rather domineering heroine, Ines Kannoyan. Sumarang is described as having eyes as large as plates and a nose "the size of two feet put together." Lam-ang easily kills him when they fight.

A unnamed two-headed giant in a Pampango tale about four blind brothers lived in a deserted house. There is also a nameless giant in a Bikol tale about "Teofilo the Hunchback and the Giant" who was taller than the house he lived in.

A Subanon tale, "The Widow's Son," tells of a giant so large and strong that he used a tree trunk as a shaft for his spear.

A Maranao tale about a sultan with a golden beard tells of unnamed giants guarding a large palace under

the sea. They were men with long, pointed teeth and sharp fingernails. Rajah Bagaram, the tale's hero, kills them all with little difficulty.

A Subanon tale tells about a hero who asked from outside a giant's home if the house owner was in and told him to come out and fight if he was. The giant in the house heard him, seized his shield and spear, and jumped out to the ground. Seeing only the man, it roared, "Where is the man who wants a fight? That thing? It is a fly."

The domicile of Philippine giants vary in both shape and location. The European giants lived far from human habitations, but Philippine giants often lived close to human settlements and villages. The bannog's nest was in a tall tree on a cliff. An Isneg tale tells about some village children entering the house of Bekat and Surab, his wife, to ask for fire to cook their food with.

Three animal friends went hunting in the woods in the Tagalog country one day and met Bungisngis, the giant fond of smiling.

Buringcantada, a giant in a Bikol tale, lived in a large house decorated with leaves and flowers. Some men entered and were in the dining room when they saw the giant get in. They climbed up into a hole in the ceiling and hid there.

Hounds in an Isneg tale barked when they reached a mountain top. The hero shouted and a giant responded. The man followed the game into a brook and saw the giant there.

The giant Gisurab in an Isneg tale lived in a cave.

The monkey-like ikugan the Manobo tell about hid in a tree above a human trail, waited for passersby, and fell on them when they came.

Two Apayao brothers captured a wild pig in the woods, prepared to cook it, and found that they had brought no match with them. One of them walked to the house of the giant Guisurab near by and asked him for fire after his brother had warned him to be careful or the giant will catch him. "Just stay below his ladder," the brother said. He got back with the fire.

Two Isneg neighbors went out to pick berries on a hill early one morning, and the basket of one of them rolled down the hill and came to the clearing of Surab and Sibbarayungan, his wife. Beside their house stood several granaries containing clothes and the human flesh they had stored there—something giants rarely relish.

The closeness of giants' habitations to human communities is indicated by a tale, "The Four Blind Brothers," where a giant is said to have lived in a deserted house.

In Batangas is told a tale about Carangal—or Span-Tall—in which a giant is said to live in a large, deserted house with windows closed. The house shook and the tiny human hero saw a giant coming up the stairs.

A Bikol tale about a hunchback and a giant says that the former had to find a place to put up for the night and came to a field. He followed a beam of light and came to a house with open windows. No one replied when he asked to be let in, and he pushed the door open and got in. Finding nobody there, he lay down and fell asleep, not knowing that this was the house of a giant.

One of three brothers lost in the woods came to an abyss. He entered it and came to a green house where lived a maiden whom a giant had been holding as a prisoner. In a similar motif from a Maranao tale, giants guarded a beautiful princess in an undersea realm where the *garuda*, an ogre that could assume the shape of a powerful bird, was holding her prisoner.

A Subanon hero got into a giant's house crowded with the men the giant had captured in battle.

What are some typical activities of Philippine giants? The bannog in a Tinguian tale carried a hunter to its nest in a tall tree and left him there for its nestlings to eat. He hid among the baby birds, eating part of the wild game the bannog brought its babies.

Certain depressions shaped like footprints in the Ilocos country, Cagayan, Pangasinan, Zambales, Bataan,

and the mountains of San Mateo, in Rizal, are said to be
the footprints of prehistoric giants. Beliefs of this sort
exist around the world.

Angngalo was of enormous size but feared the bite
of ants. In another Iloko legend about this giant, the
folk once crossed the sea on Angngalo's leg to get salt.
They filled their bags with salt, bore these on their
heads, and were walking home on the giant's out-
stretched leg when he dipped it in the sea because he
could not bear the bites of the ants swarming on it.
That, too, was how the sea became salt.

In a tale reported by Morice Vanoverbergh, two
young Isneg hunters once went to the giant Guisurab's
house to ask for fire. "Who is there?" Guisurab asked
them.

"We, sir, come to ask for fire," they replied.

"What will you do with the fire?" asked Guisurab.

"To roast a *sisiat* (a kind of insect), sir," they replied.

"I shall come and eat the sisiat, too," said Guisurab.

"We mean a *siab* (another small insect)," said the
children.

"I, too, shall eat the siab," replied Guisurab.

"We mean a *pilagay* (still another kind of insect),"
said the children.

"I shall also come and eat the pilagay," replied
Guisurab.

"We mean a wild boar," the children admitted.

"Let's go and singe it," said Guisurab, taking a live
coal and going to singe it beside the river with the
children.

The Apayao tell a cognate to that tale. A hunter kills
a wild pig and goes to Gisarub, a giant, to ask him for
fire.

"What will you do with the fire, little man?" Gisarub asked.

"To roast locusts," the man lied.

"I must come with you. I like to eat locusts," replied
Gisarub.

"I mean crabs," said the man to scare the giant since giants are said to greatly fear crabs.

"Did you say you will roast crabs?" asked Gisarub. "Crabs are even better-tasting than locusts. I will come with you."

"It's really to roast a wild pig," said the men.

"I will give you fire, little man. Carry this basket for me and show me the way. Pig's meat is the best meat for me."

The stupidity of giants is illustrated by what the two children did to Gisarub in the tale reported by Vanoverbergh. After roasting and chopping up the wild pig, Gisarub put all the meat in his burden basket. The boys then challenged him to a diving contest before they parted. They quickly replaced the meat in his basket with stones while he was under water. Then the bottom of Gisarub's wife's pot fell when he dropped the stones in his burden basket when he got home. He then hurried back to the pond with his axe, saw the boys' reflection on the water, tried to cut down the tree where they were, and cut his own leg instead.

The ikugan which the Manobo tell tales about suspended themselves by their long tails over forest trails while waiting for wayfarers to come along. When they did, they overpowered them and killed them.

The Apayao giant Sappaw wed Gungay, his own sister. Their only son wrecked their human neighbors' fences and stoned their dogs and pigs to death. The people then tried catching Sappaw with a bamboo fish trap but he tore it to pieces. They finally set up bamboo spears under the water where he often went to dive and killed him by making him spear himself.

Some of the intellectual and spiritual traits of the giants of Philippine folklore may be summed up by the statement that they had great muscular strength but were remarkably stupid. A bannog bullied six animal friends varying in size from a ponderous carabao to a tiny tortoise to give up their collective catch each had been assigned to stay behind and watch. The larger

animals failed, but when its turn to watch came, the tiny tortoise tricked the large bully into getting itself entombed in a hole it dug.

The gullibility of giants the world over illustrated by the English tale about Jack and the Beanstalk has abundant parallels in Philippine tales. Bekat, the Isneg giant, had a diving contest in a lake with two children whom she had cheated of the meat of the wild boar they had killed. The children promptly rose to breathe after Bekat dived in, put stones in her basket in place of the meat she had put in it, and climbed up into an overhanging tree. When she rose to the surface again, she carried her basket home and poured its contents into a clay pot, and the bottom of the pot fell. It then dawned on her that the children had tricked her. She went back for them, saw their reflection on the surface of the pond, dived in for them, failed to find them there, looked up, and saw them in the tree. She hurried home for her axe, walked back, and started chopping down the tree. She cut her knee instead.

In the Batangas tale, a giant pulled hair from the
head of Carangal, a span-tall child, and tied Carangal's
companion to a post with it. Carangal then induced the
giant to tie himself to the post with a strong rope and
to smear himself with wax. Carangal then set the giant
on fire. This is just one of the numerous incidents in
Philippine folklore that tell of humans outwitting giants
in their encounters. Vanoverberg's monograph on Isneg
tales has an entire section on the exploits of Little
Finger who handily outwits a variety of giants.

"Who is there?" a giant in a Tagalog tale shouted
before entering his own house. A lame man and a blind
man, who had entered the house not knowing that it
was a giant's, replied from the ceiling where they had
retreated: "We are large men." From where they were
they then dropped a ray's tail to the floor saying it was
a strand of their hair, and the giant was frightened and
fled. In a cognate Bikol tale, a man dropped a piece of
rope to the floor saying it was a strand of his head hair
and then a duck he said was a louse from his head. He
then fired a gun and said he had thumped his chest.
The giant fled in terror.

Three little children in a Tagalog tale entered the
house of the one-eyed giant Buringcantada by mistake
and hid in the ceiling—the typical Philippine home had
no other convenient compartment to hide in—when that
giant and his friends got in and began eating. The
children then yelled from the ceiling:

> *Tawi cami*
> *Sa quisame*
> *Que masaran*
> *Na ulaman!*
> (A corrupt mix of Tagalog and
> Spanish meaning:
> We are people
> In the ceiling.
> How nice the viand!)

The giant was infuriated by the evidence of intruders and said, "If you are as large as you say, let me see a strand of your hair!"

They dropped a piece of rope to the floor.

The giant then asked to see a tooth from their mouth, and they dropped the head of an axe.

Then the giant asked them to thump their chest. They beat on a bass drum and the giant fled.

In a Bagobo tale recorded in an extended monograph by Laura Watson Benedict, a giant saw a monkey gathering vines. The monkey said it needed the vines to protect itself from an imminent typhoon. The giant begged the monkey to tie him to a tree so that the typhoon would not blow him away. The monkey did so and then thrashed him without mercy. Later the monkey told the giant to strike a hive of wild bees. It did so and the bees swarmed on him and stung him. The giant was killed when the monkey lured it to enter the open mouth of a large crocodile which the monkey said was the king's room he had been assigned to guard.

Legends and tales about giants and ogres chiefly serve for emotional release for those who listen to them. Children repeatedly and almost invariably best want giants and ogres in folktales. These triumphs help release emotional tension born of the listeners' handicap as puny creatures comparatively powerless but by use of their superior wit and skill can easily beat their hulking but feebleminded adversaries.

The Merfolk

The Maiden and the Merman

SOLANG WAS PRETTY, but she was near thirty and a man was still to claim her. She and her mother walked to the river with the week's wash one morning. They soaked the clothes in a basin at the edge of the water, rubbed a cake of soap on the clothes till the suds billowed, and spread them on the pebbled bank to bleach.

Then they the dipped themselves in the water, soaping their hair with thin lye from the rice straw they burned on the bank. After that the mother wiped her hair dry and lay down for a nap under a tree while Solang paddled about, splashing water on the clothes in the sun now and then to keep them steaming.

After a while she thought she heard someone call her by name. She looked, and there, waist deep in the river, stood a man.

"Uncle Asiong!" she said.

She turned to tell her mother, but she was still asleep. Then she looked again, and her jaw fell, for he had turned into a smiling youth, his handsome face, shoulders, and arms gleaming in the sun.

"Come here," said the stranger. "Come."

"I will! I will!" Solang exclaimed with a giggle.

"What did you say, Solang?" her mother asked, awakened by her voice and propping up her head with one hand.

"Oh, nothing, Mother," she replied.

"I thought I heard you," her mother said.

"Well, I spoke to him," she said, and with her pursed lips she pointed to the handsome stranger, but he was gone.

The mother rose and waded to where Solang stood in the water. "Are you all right?" she asked.

"Uncle Asiong was in the middle of the river," said Solang. "I turned, and when I looked back he was gone, and a handsome stranger stood where he had been."

"You must be tired," her mother said. "Why don't you lie down and get yourself some rest?"

"I'm all right, Mother," Solang said.

They beat the clothes on the crown of a gray rock that stood out of the water, rinsed them, and laid them out to dry on the sand. Under the tree they ate their lunch of rice and roasted river fish they had brought along wrapped in banana leaves. Then they lay down to let their meal settle. After a while they got up, gathered the dried clothes, and headed for home.

Solang's father fetched an old widow who helped the ailing with muttered chants and made offerings to the creatures of the dark with whom it was said she had secret dealings. Solang's mother told the widow what had happened at the river.

"What your daughter saw," said the widow, nodding, "was an *ugkoy*. He wanted her to go with him."

Muttering secret phrases, the widow burned some guava leaves in a clay brazier and made Solang inhale the smoke from these. Solang calmed down and was soon asleep on her sleeping mat.

Solang's parents breathed easier while she slept. But they woke up next morning to find her missing. She was not in the kitchen or in the yard, and she was not at the village store. They traced her footprints to the river, and where she and her mother had washed clothes the day before, she stood earnestly talking to no one. They asked what was with her, and she replied that the handsome stranger had come to the village for her before dawn and urged her to follow him. Her face had a strange glow as she spoke, and there was a mirthless smile on her lips and a wild light in her eyes. She made a caper at the edge of the water like a dancing girl.

They led her home against her will and put her in bed. She could get no sleep and made swimming motions on her sleeping mat. "Water, water!" she sang. "How wonderful to be in the water with your man!"

The widow healer was sent for again. She came, burned more leaves and threw in some chicken feathers on the burning coals. They burned these under the floor and beside her mat.

But she never got over what she insisted she saw. She grew more restless and haggard each day, and then she seemed to hear no other voice but that of her merman lover.

Her parents awoke one morning to find her gone. With their neighbors they traced her footprints to the river as before. She was not there, and they followed the winding stream to where it joined the sea.

For two days they went out each morning early and followed the river down to the sea, but they failed to find her. Then, on the third day, they found her where the river met the sea, and she moved every which way the water moved. Her long tresses pointed in all directions like the

fronds of a seaweed, and her arms were stretched out as if
she had leaped forward to embrace her lover.

"She followed her merman," the old widow said with
a sigh, "but he refused to take her into his realm."

THE WORD *merfolk* means 'people of the sea'. There are
numerous Philippine legends about merfolk, but their
local names are few. It may be that the Spanish name—
sirena—superseded most of the local names, which
include:

kataw ('one like us') — West Visayan
magindara—Bikol
siukoy—Tagalog, Visayan
ugkoy—Tagalog, Visayan

As in European folklore, there are fewer mermen than
mermaids in Philipine folklore. Mermaids are beautiful
young women above the waist and fish below. Mermen
are good-looking young men from head to waist and fish
below that. Mermaids have long hair, a light complexion,
and sweet voices, and mermen have short, curly hair and
sunburnt skin. Both look like attractive youths above the
waist, but their lower bodies are those of scaly fish. Since
there are far fewer mermen than mermaids, it may be
inferred that these creatures are polygamous but no
legends to this effect are told.

Unlike in Europe where merfolk inhabit salt water
almost exclusively, Philippine mermaids and mermen
abound in rivers, lakes, and the basins of waterfalls as well
as bays, gulfs, and seas. A mermaid was often reported to
have been heard wailing in distress—its method of
attracting its prey—at night in a stream at the edge of this
writer's hometown during the rainy season. When the
rains poured and the river leaped over a culvert across the
stream, the farmers had to cross over from their outlying
fields on foot at the end of the day, and their greatest fear
was not that of drowning but of the mermaid they
believed lying in wait for them in the water.

The basin of Botocan Falls, close to Manila, is reported

to be inhabited by a mermaid although the falls has long
been harnessed to generate electricity for the metropolis.
The Pampanga River just north of Manila is also said to
have mermaids lying in wait for unwary swimmers, and
so are rivers throughout the country, from the Cagayan in
the North of Luzon to the Maguindanao in the South.

Merfolk are said to have beautiful underwater homes
with walls bright with gold and precious stones. They do
not kill the children and youth they capture. They raise
them in their underwater realm instead, and somehow
their human captives do not drown. They marry them
when they grow up. They entice children to get into the
water with their enchanting voices. They sing sweet songs
or plaintively lament to draw youngsters to them. When
someone they like goes near, they make the water
suddenly rise and grab him or her. They then take their
captive to their underwater realm.

Merfolk are reported to march at the tail ends of
religious processions and try to entice boys and girls to the
river with them. This belief may have been invented to
make children join religious processions promptly and

avoid the tail ends of processions. Merfolk are also said to join crowds of people and whisper to their prospective victim: "Please walk me to the edge of the water."

They are said to ask those they capture what they are fond of eating. When asked this question, one should avoid saying he is fond of meat or fish, otherwise the merman or mermaid will drown him or her for eating part of its body. Nor should one reply that he likes to eat greens with curly tips, for merfolk have curly hair. Legends are told of many a river where a mermaid takes a child, known by the folk as a "tribute" to her. The victim is known as *naserena* ('taken by a mermaid'), and the water where it happened is *awakan* in Southern Mindanao.

A telltale trait of merfolk is their strong fishy smell.

The Visayan *kataw* is said to be a voluptuous maiden from head to waist, light-complexioned, and with wavy long hair. She has been seen singing on a rock out at sea and drying her long hair in the sun, and a dugong sunning itself on a rock at sea would closely resemble such a woman in silhouette. The mermaid entices fishermen who go near her, grabs them, and takes them to

her underwater home and marries him if a man or raises
him to manhood if a child and eventually weds him. By
her magic power her human captive does not drown.

Like the other mermaids, the *magindara* of the
Bikolanos is a beautiful maiden above the waist and a fish
below. A young man went to live with a magindara in her
cave under the sea and was never seen again.

The *mambubûno*, believed in by the Zambale, is said to
have twin tails instead of a single tail. These are covered
with dark, slimy fish scales in the males. Instead of being
dark, the twin tails of the female mambubûno are said to
be covered with scales of varied bright colors. The
mambubûno may be found in a brook or river with a cave
under its bank, and its home is bright with gold and
precious stones. A mermaid marries the man she has
enticed to go with her to her realm and keeps him as her
prisoner without his knowing it. He may visit his folks if
he promises to return. Should she catch him trying to
escape, she will drown him and he will be found seated at
the bottom of the water or squatting stiff there. If she lets
him visit his folks, he will find them all aged or dead and

the neighbors may not believe where he says he has been
to all these years. That life with the mambubûno is blissful
is indicated by the belief that a day with her seems a year
in the world of men.

Sirena is the most common name of mermaids in the
Philippines, a Spanish term which superseded many of the
native names of the creature after the Spanish conquest.

It is said that one who has a birthmark on his eyeball is
likely to see a sirena.

A mermaid's hair is long and her voice is magically
sweet. She makes children go to her by singing. At night a
man may hear a sirena wailing in distress in the water and
go down and try to help her. Then she will make the water
suddenly rise and get him.

Visayans call the mermaid *ugkoy* and some Tagalogs
call the merman *siukoy*. A siukoy's skin is sunburned and
hairy and his head hair copper-colored and wavy but
relatively short.

Merfolk are said to frequent flooded rivers, floating
quietly on the water to attract attention with their physical
beauty. When they see youngsters swimming in the water,
they pull them down by their legs and take them to their
home.

The belief in merfolk has made Filipinos fear rivers
and seas although their country consists of over 7,000
islands. And they commonly resort to dynamite fishing,
one of the most harmful ways to catch fish, since dynamite
kills fish fry as well as fishermen.

Homer is the author of the most famous story about
sirens in literature. In the *Odyssey*, he tells of the
enchantress Circe, who has charmed and held Odysseus
and his men prisoners in her cave for many years but now
lets them go, warns him that his ship will sail through a
narrow strait inhabited by the sirens—beautiful sea
nymphs with magically sweet voices. She tells Odysseus
to stop his men's ears with wax before they enter the strait
and that if he wants to hear the sirens' voices, he should
leave his ears open but have himself tied to the mast and
order his men to ignore his command to be released as

they sail past the sirens. They get there and Odysseus'
men admire the beautiful sirens but do not hear their
magic voices. Odysseus hears as well as sees them but his
men ignore his orders to release him, and they all escape
from the mermaids.

Heinrich Heine wrote a poem about a mermaid
singing in the river Rhine—a rare case of siren in soft
water in European literature.

Hans Christian Andersen, the Danish writer of
fascinating fairy tales, tells a touching story of a mermaid
that falls in love with a human sailor aboard his ship. She
follows the ship wherever it sails but is never even noticed
by him and her heart breaks and she dies. A bronze statue
of her is shown seated on a rock by a river in Copenhagen.
It was recently mutilated by a vandal but was promptly
restored.

"The Forsaken Merman," a poem by Matthew Arnold,
tells a touching story of a village girl who went to live
under the sea with a merman and they had children. Upon
her insistence, he let her return to her home so that she
may attend a church service. She is slow to return, and the
merman and their children swim ashore and call out to
her from outside the church walls, unable to enter. She
does not hear them and never goes back to the sea, and
that is Arnold's spoof on traditional religion.

A mermaid legend used to be told by this writer's
mother, a descendant of immigrants from Paoay, Ilocos
Norte, folk who pioneered in southern Zambales at the
beginning of the nineteenth century. She evidently told it
to warn her children to avoid going to the river that was
within shouting distance from this writer's gate. The
legend went this way:

The Boy and the Mermaid

A little boy was gathering pebbles at the edge of the river one day when he saw a beautiful woman in the water. She smiled sweetly at him and said. "Come here, Son, and I will tell you a wonderful story."

He was attracted by her sweet smile, her golden voice, and her long curls and walked to her. As soon as his feet touched the water, the river suddenly rose and he found himself in her arms.

"Let me go! Let me go!" screamed the boy.

She held him firmly and said, "Be quiet and I shall take you to a wonderful world you have never seen before."

"My folks will be looking for me!" said the boy.

"A wonderful new world is waiting for you," she said, diving into the water.

The boy saw that from the waist down her body was covered with fish scales, and it tapered into twin fins flipping from side to side as the two of them went through the water with little effort.

Soon they reached the sea, and the coral beds shone and painted fish flashed by as they swam through the clear water. At last they came to a beautiful house at the bottom of the sea. They entered a door and came into a gorgeous hall. The doors and windows had jambs of black coral, and the floors and furniture were gold accented with rubies and pearls.

They sat down, and the mermaid—for a mermaid she was—asked, "Tell me what greens you ate in the world of men. Did you eat boiled squash tops with long tendrils? Did you eat fern tips?"

"We never ate those things," he replied, remembering it told that mermaids asked these questions to test those they captured.

"Did you eat fish?" she asked.

"We never ate fish," he replied.

"What about meat?"

"No meat."

"What did you eat then?"

"Only rice, salt, and fruit," he replied.

"That's fine," said the mermaid smiling. "Had you said you ate squash tendrils and young fern shoots with curly tips, you would have become my enemy. Tendrils and fern tips are part of a mermaid's hair. And since half of my body is that of a fish and half is the body of a human, I am a mix of both fish and people. He who eats fish and meat eats me and is my foe."

"Please say when I can go home," said the boy.

"This is your home now," she replied. "Let me show you around," she added, taking him by the hand, and they went around in the house. The first two rooms each contained a bed of gold with canopies studded with pearl. In the dining room were golden trays and porcelain ware.

The mermaid turned to the boy and said, "This is your home. Everything in it is yours." Then she added: "I shall leave you awhile. Remember, this is your home. Enjoy it."

She briefly disappeared into the back of the house and then returned and left through the front door.

The boy tried to enjoy himself but kept on thinking of his folks.

The mermaid returned at the end of the day with good things to eat. The boy pretended to enjoy the food and she offered him more of it, but he could eat little.

Then night came and she went to sleep in her golden bed. He, too, lay down in his bed in the next room but turned from side to side all night and had little sleep.

Before she left again next day, she stepped into the back of the house as she had done the day before and then left through the front door. "Enjoy yourself, eat lots of food, and grow quickly into a man," she said, leaving him.

She promptly returned at the end of the day and they had a sumptuous meal and then went into their separate beds.

This went on day after day, and the boy kept longing for home.

He wondered why the mermaid went to the back of the house before she left each day. Was there a secret door she kept him from knowing about? He went to the rear of the house after she left to see if he could find a way of escape. He was feeling on the back wall one day when he felt a part of it give under pressure. He pushed harder and discovered a door so well hidden that he could not have distinguished it from the rest of the wall had he not pressed it. He was about to enter the door when he heard the mermaid turn the lock on the front door. He barely had time to shut the secret door quietly and go and meet her in the hall.

"Have you been enjoying yourself today?" she asked.

He nodded without a word.

"It's dark at the back of the house," she said. "Never go there."

He nodded again, but as soon as she left next day, he rushed to the rear of the house and opened the secret door. He entered a little room and saw a porcelain jar standing on the floor. He looked into it and found a golden bowl floating there. It dawned on him that the mermaid bathed herself in the liquid before leaving for the world of men. He dipped the bowl and poured the liquid on his head and shoulders.

At once a trapdoor opened beneath his feet. He ran out, followed a sandy path into the world bright with sunshine and loud with the singing of birds. Soon he reached the river bank where the mermaid had captured him.

His folks and their neighbors were overjoyed when he got home and told them where he had been. They gave a big feast to celebrate his return.

For many nights after that, the villagers near the river heard a voice wailing plaintively at the stream. "That's the

mermaid," the mothers told their children. "She is calling
for her escaped prisoner."

"Never play near the river again or the mermaid will
get you," added the grandmothers.

The Ogres

The Scold and the Ogre

HE LOOKED LIKE a large man with hard, curved fingernails, ferocious teeth, and massive shoulders and legs. He lived in the dark woods of the Cordilleras. He heated pieces of iron in his smithy under a thatched grass roof and beat them into bows and arrows, axes, and bolos. He dipped them in water to temper them. Then he disguised himself as a good-looking youth, walked into the villages in the lowlands, and exchanged his iron wares with farm products and other things he carried home on his shoulders.

Four little brave boys hunting for deer wandered into his part of the woods one day. Under dark trees they rapped on his door wondering who lived there.

"Come right in," he said, meeting them as a handsome man. He was holding his blacksmith's tools.

The boys entered, and his wife gave them food to eat and water to drink. Then he led them downstairs, suddenly pushed them into the bellows of his idle old smithy, turned the heavy latch, and left them screaming there.

He let them out at mealtime, fed them well, and left them to play in his yard. Then when night came, he fed them well and shut them inside the bellows again.

This went on day after day. Whenever he left to go out trading or hunting, he put them back in the bellows and only let them out to eat and play when he got back.

He forgot to latch the bellows door before leaving one day. As soon as his back was turned, the two boys pushed open the door and ran till they lost their breath. They briefly sat down panting and then ran again. At last they reached their village far down in the valley. Their folks shouted with joy to see them back and gave a big feast to celebrate their return. The four boys never entered those woods again.

A young farmer and his wife lived in a village some woods and meadows away from the forest where lived Inlablabbuut—for that was who the blacksmith was. The farmer was a quiet and hardworking man, and she was pretty but a terrible scold, often railing at him with her sharp tongue. He worked alone on his farm up in the rice terraces all day, growing rice, camotes, peas, and greens. Whenever he came home each evening, it was her habit to complain that there was not enough to eat in the house. "And I have no nice dresses and beads to wear," she would scream at him.

"I work hard, dear wife," he would reply. "But our farm is small and I can raise only what I can."

"Do something about it," she would reply crossly.

This went on until finally, after another severe scolding from her, he put his things in his burden basket, walked away, and never returned.

A tall young stranger with a fair complexion came into
the village near the end of the day soon after. He walked
before the woman's home and smiled pleasantly at her
while she sat at her doorstep in the sunset. She smiled
back and told him to drop in. He did, and they sat smiling
at each other. Finally he said he loved her, she said she
loved him, too, and they lived as husband and wife. He
had brought nothing with him, and they ate the food her
husband left before he departed.

"Come home with me," he then told her.

"Where is your home?" she asked.

"Just beyond those woods yonder," he replied,
pointing in the distance. "Put your things in a basket and
let's go."

She put on her prettiest dress and her sparkling
jewelry and placed a few extra garments in a basket. Then
she bolted the windows and door, and the two of them
were on their way.

"It's nice and cool out here," she said, walking behind
him up and down a forest trail.

He looked back at her with a pleasant smile and
walked on in silence.

"Is your place far from here?" she asked after they had walked a little more.

"It's just a little farther on," he replied.

They left the woods and came to a green meadow where wild flowers bloomed and birds sang in the trees. They walked across the meadow and soon entered a second wood. Here the trees stood closer together, and their tops were high up in the sky.

He turned to her and said, "Wait for me here a while."

"Where are you going?" she asked.

"Just behind those trees," he replied.

"Why?"

"To answer the call of nature," he replied, walking off. She sat down at the foot of a tree and watched him go.

When he came back, she was astounded to see that he had grown much taller. His legs had become longer and larger and were each covered with coarse hair. His feet, too, had grown larger and thicker, and his toenails stuck out.

"What has happened to your legs?" she asked, greatly disturbed.

"They grow larger when I enter these woods," he replied with a smile. "Don't you worry. They will grow smaller again."

They walked on and soon came to another green meadow bright with flowers and loud with the singing of birds. They crossed the meadow slowly because she stopped now and then to admire the beauty of the things around her.

They then entered another wood where the trees were thick and tall. Now he turned to her and said, "Wait for me here a while. I won't be long."

"Where are you going this time?" she asked.

"Just behind those trees to answer the call of nature," he replied and walked away.

She sat down on a raised root and waited for him.

When he came back, she was more disturbed than before. His shoulders, body, and arms had grown larger, too. A thick mat of hair covered his chest and forearms, and hard, pointed nails were at the tips of his fingers and thumbs.

"What has happened to you?" she asked, more troubled than before.

"I become this way when I walk through these woods," he said. "But don't you worry. My body will grow as small and handsome as before when we get out of the woods. Come, let's go on."

They walked into another green meadow bright with flowers and loud with the singing of birds. She almost forgot his strange transformations when she beheld the beauty of the things around her.

They left the meadow and soon entered another wood. The branches of the trees and the stems and leaves of vines climbing them darked the forest.

"I will leave you one last time," he said. "Wait for me."

"Be sure it's the last time," she said, starting to be annoyed.

He smiled and disappeared behind the trees. The low, mysterious calls of creatures she had never heard before came to her ears and she grew afraid.

He soon came back, and now his head had swelled and grown ugly with fierce eyes and a large flat nose. Sharp teeth stuck out of his large mouth, his ears flapped on both sides of his head when he turned, and coarse black hair covered his head and face. He had become the ogre Inlablabbuut.

She panicked and tried to run away from him, but he snatched her in his large hands and then devoured her. Her bones crackled between his teeth as he chewed her. Then he belched with satisfaction and walked to his home deep in those dark woods.

THE CANNIBAL monster in the foregoing legend is an ogre—a man-eating giant of which the following are Philippine examples:

    alan—Tinguian

    Berberoka—Apayao

    busaw as a man eater—Bagobo, Bukidnon, Mandaya

garuda—Maranao
Inlablabbuut—Ifugao
siring—Bagobo
ta-awi—Maranao

Ogres are cannibal giants of folklore. Like the giants, they are hominoid in shape. Giants live far from human communities while ogres live near human settlements, assuming human shape and often interacting with the folk.

The names of some Philippine ogres, like those of some of the giants, are capitalized and printed in Roman type in the literature since they look like people at least part of the time. They live in frontier areas such as the Cordilleras in Northern Luzon and close to forest clearings in Mindanao. No ogres have been reported from the more urbanized areas in the country.

Philippine ogres change their shapes not only to human but to animal forms as well to disguise themselves. Some ogres have kindly wives who conceal human stragglers from them and then help the stragglers escape.

In spite of their fearful habits and appearance, ogres are so feebleminded that human children and in one case even a cat outwit them.

The *alan* is an ogre much feared by the Tinguian of the Cordillera range in Northern Luzon. He prefers human flesh to fish or animal meat for food. His skin resembles the rough hide of a carabao, and he has long arms and sharp fingernails. His hands and feet point the other way around so that he has gone the other way when his footprints point this way. The alan lives in large trees deep in the woods, sleeping head down like a bat in a concealed position and goes out hunting for prey at night. An alan disguised as a human villager knew that an expectant mother was fond of sour green mangoes. He gave her these in return for which she recklessly promised to give him her baby if a boy. It was a boy, and the alan came and carried it away wrapped in a kerchief.

There are said to be large jars containing beads and gold pieces in the alan's house deep in the woods. These he took from the people he ate. He locates people by sniffing like a dog and saying he smells the blood of a man, much as the English giant that said, "Fi-fee-fo-fum, I smell the blood of an Englishman!" The alan makes himself also look like a domesticated chicken and then freely goes about in human villages. He also turns himself into a fresh-water fish to hide his identity.

The Apayaos greatly fear Berberoka, another Northern Luzon ogre. He has a habit of lying down across a stream full of fish, and his body grows bigger and bigger as he drinks the water. When the village folk come down to gather fish in the dried river bed, he suddenly gets up and gathers those caught in the rushing waters. But Berberoka is cowardly, running away in terror when pinched by a crab.

Binobaan is an ogre among the Ifugao, builders of those splendid rice terraces tourists rhapsodize about. Binobaan's voice is thunderous, and he lives in the woods. His house is roofed with thatched leaves, and there he

stores rice heads in bundles. When the bundles are dry he
pounds and hulls them. He cooks the rice in a large clay
pot before each mealtime. Disguised as a man, Binobaan
invites lost hunters to share his food. He gives them
fermented rice—*bubud*—to eat, and when they get
inebriated from eating too much of it, they are helpless
and he devours them. Binobaan's ogre wife is kindly,
however, and hides human stragglers from her husband.
When he enters his house and says he smells a man, she
replies that there is no man in the house. He then eats the
meal she has cooked for him, and he goes out hunting
again and his wife feeds the frightened stragglers and
shows them their way home.

The man-eating *busaw* terrorizes the Bagobos,
Bukidnons, and Mandayas in the jungles of Central and
Eastern Mindanao. A female busaw has a single eye just
above her nose. A busaw chief has a horn of ivory on top
of his head. He lives in a large house on a wide fertile
plain, and around it his busaw followers live in smaller
huts. His men raise bananas, taro, and yams. They also
raise carabaos, and their premises are littered with the

bones of the people and wild game they have devoured. One busaw chases people by putting on wings and flying after them.

Other busaw live in large trees in the jungle. Their coarse hair swarms with lice and worms. A busaw assumed the form of a man one night and walked to a house. Only the housewife was there, her husband having gone out fishing. A cat sitting before the closed door refused to let the busaw in—for unlike the cats in European folklore, felines in Philippine folk traditional lore are faithful to their human masters and will have no traffic with demonological beings such as ogres and witches. The busaw asked the cat to let him in. "I will let you in if you first count my hair," replied the cat. The busaw started counting the cat's hair and was almost through when the cat suddenly ruffled it and the busaw had to begin counting all over again. This went on and on until the dawn broke and the busaw fled to the woods without getting in.

Still another busaw lived in the dark forest close to a clearing where a man grew upland rice. The man sent his little daughter to the clearing to scare off the sparrows that were eating the ripening grain. She sat in the shade beside the clearing shaking the twine with which she had tied noise-making objects hung on the line. The noise attracted a busaw living in an adjoining forest. It walked to the clearing, found the girl, and asked her to go with it to its house. She went and there the busaw had her remove the large lice that swarmed in its coarse head hair.

After she had done so, the busaw put her in its burden basket, put the basket on its head, and walked out. On the way the busaw sat down to rest, and the girl quietly climbed out of the basket, put stones in it, and said she was ready to proceed. The busaw rose and walked on thinking the girl was in the basket.

She climbed to the top of a betel nut tree and the busaw, realizing that she was not in his basket and coming back to find her, saw her up in the tree. It climbed a betel nut tree beside her tree and said, "Tree, tree, go up, go up."

The tree went up, but the girl told her tree to go down while the tree the busaw was on was up. Seeing her down, the busaw told its tree to go down, too, but then the girl told her tree to go up. This went on and on until the busaw grew dizzy, fell down, and died. The girl then walked home.

The *siring* is much feared by the Bagobo of Southeastern Mindanao. It has a fearful look and has sharp fingernails. It lives on a tall mountain and lures hunters to its lair. Like the tikbalang of the Tagalog, it makes itself look exactly like a wanderer's father and then leads him to its tree house and feeds him with brown rice that is really worms. It is scared by red pepper, and this helps explain why many Philippine folk like hot peper in their food. The belief that the creature feeds those it has lured into its domain brown rice also helps explain why Filipinos prefer highly polished, vitamin B_1-poor rice to unpolished rice in their diet, thus predisposing themselves to beriberi.

The *ta-awi* is much feared by the Maranao of Central Mindanao. It is an ugly monster that can fly faster than the

wind, the sweep of its wings making forest trees below its line of flight bend. It enters and attacks human communities and devours the inhabitants raw. But it spares pretty maidens and imprisons them in its home on top of a high mountain. A ta-awi was fatally wounded by a human hero and asked him to open its stomach. He did so, and out fell the eyeballs of the people the monster had devoured. The hero then restored the owners of the eyes to life.

The Maranaos have the best developed folk literature among all Philippine groups. Their long folk epic—or *Darangen*—tells of the heroic exploits of Bantugen and is the finest in this genre in the entire country. It was taken down in the 1930s by Maranao researchers and then translated into English iambic pentameters by Frank C. Laubach, an American Presbyterian missionary to the Maranaos and the resident minister of the Marawi—then Dansalan—Protestant Church. The Maranaos themselves, however, have not been satisfied with the Laubach translation. They have tape-recorded the epic, and press reports have it that it is scheduled for publication in ten volumes of text in 1987 by the Mindanao State University. An English translation of the material is underway there, too.

In Indonesian folklore, the *garuda* is a winged god adapted by the Indonesian Airways System as its trade name. This is a mythical bird figure in the *Darangen* and in at least two Maranao legends. The garuda is a fearful ogre in these legends while it is a beneficial god in Hindu mythology, giving support to the theory that gods tend to deteriorate in proportion to the distance from their place of origin. In Maranao folklore the creature is a frightful giant man-eater with sharp teeth protruding from its mouth like sharp knives. In pursuit of its human prey it turns into a powerful bird. The trees below are uprooted in its flight, and it can carry six men in its talons.

In an extended Maranao tale, a Sultan who had a golden beard was fond of combing it in his garden each morning. A little bird flew by and snatched off some of the

sultan's beard and flew off with it. The sultan summoned
his three sons, told them what had happened, and ordered
them to catch the bird and bring it to him.

The three sons mounted their steeds next morning and
waited for the bird to appear. It came, snatched off more
of the sultan's golden beard, and flew away. They gave
chase but gave up when it flew out to sea. The two elder
brothers wanted to return home, but the youngest
suggested that they follow the bird on a boat instead. Next
morning when the bird flew in and snatched off more of
the sultan's golden beard, the three princes pursued it on a
sailboat. They soon lost sight of the bird but sailed on in
the direction it had taken.

After several days they came to a column of smoke
rising from the sea. They sailed closer to it and saw that
the smoke came out of a large hole in the water. They
looked from the edge of the hole but failed to see how far
down it went. Then they tied lengths of rope to a basket
and lowered the eldest brother in the hole after he had
told them to pull him out when he shook the rope. He
shook the rope soon after being lowered and was
promptly pulled out.

They then lowered the second eldest brother and he,
too, soon shook the rope and was pulled out.

Then the two failed brothers lowered Rajah Bagaram,
the youngest, and he went down and down and down
until he reached the bottom of the hole. There he came to a
beautiful land, green with meadows, bright with flowers,
and loud with the singing of birds. He walked and walked
and came to a handsome house. Large dogs with long
sharp teeth met him at the gate. He drew his sword, slew
them all, and entered. He was met by a beautiful maiden,
and he asked who she was.

"I am Princess Gonongleda," she replied.

"And why are you here?" he asked.

"I am the prisoner of the garuda," she said. "He
devoured my parents in the upper world and then
brought me here as his prisoner."

He asked if she knew about the bird that had been

snatching off his father's beard. She replied that she knew
of no such bird but suggested that he proceed to the next
house down the road where the garuda had another
beautiful captive princess who might know.

Rajah Bagaram thanked her for the information, told
her to wait for him, and walked on.

He came to another beautiful house. Giants with long
teeth met him at the gate, and Rajah Bagaram slew them
all, entered, and was met by another beautiful maiden.

"I am Princess Intantiaya," replied she to his question,
"a captive of the garuda." She added that the monster had
imprisoned her there after devouring her parents in the
world of men.

He asked if she knew about the beard-snatching bird,
and she replied she didn't but added that there was
another beautiful princess imprisoned by the garuda in a
house farther down the road. She warned him, however,
not to go there, for the garuda itself guarded the princess.

Rajah Bagaram nevertheless went and soon came to
another beautiful house. No one stopped him at the gate,
but a maiden even more beautiful than the first two met
him. He asked her name and she replied that she was
Princess Rasagadang.

Then he asked if she knew anything about the beard-
snatching bird, and she replied, "Yes. I am that bird."

Asked why she had done it, she replied, "It was the
only way to get someone to come and rescue my two
companions and me."

A fearful sound was presently heard, and Princess
Rasagadang told him to hide because the garuda was
coming. "I had hoped someone would come and rescue
us," she added, "but now that you are here and the
monster is coming, I am very much afraid. Hide!"

He replied that he had never hidden from anyone in
his life and was not going to hide now.

"But you do not know the garuda," she said. "The
sound you hear is from its wings as it flies over the
forest."

"The more terrible the enemy," he replied, "the greater
my victory."

She volunteered to hide him somewhere but he told
her not to worry about him.

The garuda presently entered, making the house shake
under its tread. Its wings turned into powerful arms and it
now looked like a giant monster terrible to behold. To the
floor it dropped the bodies of several men it had brought
home to eat and then growled, "I smell a man!"

Rajah Bagaram met it and said, "Smell all you can
now, for I am the last man you will ever smell."

"You are a bold little fellow," the garuda said. "I shall
gladly have you for supper."

The two fought. Rajah Bagaram, seeming to be
everywhere at the same time, skipped around the
lumbering monster and stabbed it with the serpentine
blade of his sword.

With a heavy thud the garuda finally fell to the floor
and Rajah Bagaram cut off its head.

Then Rajah Bagaram turned to Princess Rasagadang
and said, "Now I propose to carry out my father's orders."

She replied that she would be very glad to go with him
but asked that they also drop in for the two other
princesses.

"That I shall gladly do," he replied.

On the way to the bottom of the pit they stopped for
Princess Intantiaya and Princess Gonongleda. They first
asked Princess Rasagadang to sit in the basket. She did so,
and they shook the rope and it was quickly pulled up.

The two brothers at the mouth of the pit had waited
wondering what had happened to Rajah Bagaram. Both
fell in love with Princess Rasagadang as soon as they saw
her. "I saw her first and she is mine," said the younger
prince.

"I am older than you and have first claim on her,"
replied the other.

They were about to fight when Princess Rasagadang
told them to lower the rope for another princess.

The older prince thought no other woman could be as
beautiful as this. "Wait for the next one," he said. "This
princess is mine."

They lowered and pulled out the rope, and Princess
Intantiaya soon stepped out. The younger prince gladly
claimed her and they lowered the rope again.

When they pulled it out and saw Princess Gonongleda,
they both claimed her, too. They lowered the basket a
fourth time, however, and when they pulled it out and
saw Rajah Bagaram coming up in it, they cut the rope and
the basket fell out of sight with him in it. Then the two
wicked brothers took the three princesses home, warning
them to tell no one about what they had done to their
brother.

"Where is Rajah Bagaram?" the sultan asked when
they arrived home.

"He fell into the sea," the two wicked brothers replied.
"We tried hard to rescue him but he drowned and we left
him in the sea." They added that they each wanted to
marry the princesses whom they had brought home, the
elder claiming Princess Rasagadang as well as Princess
Intantiaya since he was the older.

Priests were sent for and the wedding rites were started. But the princesses did not reply when asked if they were willing to marry the princes, and the weddings could not go on.

Meanwhile, the moment Rajah Bagaram was lifted out of the garuda's realm, the water around the pit rushed in from the bottom up, keeping the basket containing him afloat, and he fell harmlessly on the sea. A large fish sidled to him. He climbed to its back and it carried him to the shore. There he thanked the fish and walked and walked until he met a kindly old woman who showed him the way to his father's sultanate.

When he reached his native land, the wicked brothers saw him coming and fled. Then the three princesses told the sultan what the two had done to their brother.

The sultan sent warriors out after the two wicked princes and captured them. The kind-hearted Rajah Bagaram begged the sultan to forgive them when they were brought to the palace. The sultan forgave them reluctantly, the three marriages were performed, and years later when the sultan was full of years, he made Rajah Bagaram sultan after him and Princess Rasagadang sultana.

The Vampires

The Taxi Dancer Who
Took Off at Midnight

HE WAS A COLLEGE freshman in 1930. He studied his lessons and slept next to the roof of an abandoned garage that was a distant cousin's quarters ten meters from the corner of Dakota, now Jorge Bocobo, and Tennessee, now Leon Guinto Streets. He paid ₱15 a month for room and board, and his laundry cost ₱12 a month, and that included two suits of white drill, the required classroom wear.

His bed was unvarnished wood with rattan floor strips woven into octagonal eyelets and stretched on a steel frame with waterpipe legs. The bed also cost ₱15 at a furniture shop on Dart Street, in Paco. His round table of tanguile wood still stands in the reading room in his Quezon City home, and all his five children, four of them with M.A., M.S., and Ph.D. degrees from American state universities, have used it, too. It cost ₱15.

At the end of each month he would knock at the door of a handsome two-story house below the Luneta Hotel on San Luis—now T.M. Kalaw Street—at sundown, be let in by a maid, and quietly walk up an elegant stairway where a handsome grandfather clock chimed off the hours. He would then enter a small room on the roof of the house, which belonged to a Spaniard with a Filipina wife for whom his uncle, Paulino Sahagun, collected house rent in the city and who gave the uncle free quarters and meals as

well as a salary. He would be handed his monthly
allowance of ₱40 all told, the aggregate amount of which
he was to succeed in paying back after he eventually
landed a job, though it was to take four years, from his
monthly salary of from ₱87 to ₱130.

The street car line was two blocks from the campus,
and the fare was just three centavos, but he walked, he
said for exercise but it was really to save the amount.

In short, he had the eye of the realist born of that tough
time of the great economic depression of the middle
thirties.

His library readings in his sophomore year had grown
too heavy for him to live so far from the campus and he
asked his uncle to allow him to live nearer the university.
He found that room and board at a rooming house a block
from the campus cost just ₱15 a month, too, and he moved
there though his laundry continued to be done at the old
place.

He now shared a room with Cardo, an engineering
student from his hometown and brother to a provincial
politician. Cardo knew night life in the city and one Friday
evening after he received ₱15 for a couple of poems
published in the *Philippine Magazine,* a monthly owned and
edited by A. V. H. Hartendorp, a former psychology
teacher from Colorado who became enamored of things

Philippine, the two of them boarded a street car and got off near a suburban cabaret where a dance could be had for ten centavos. From the madame at the gate he bought ten tickets on punched strips. That meant lots of dancing, but he bought another ten and then another still, and he waltzed, one-stepped, and foxtrotted it with a girl with rosy cheeks and a slim figure who held him tight and rested her lips on his neck while they danced. He tried to make conversation, but she evidently had just recently arrived from the country since she knew next to no Tagalog or English. All he learned from her was that she came from an obscure Visayan village.

She had a habit of briefly leaving the dancehall at midnight—to powder her face, neck, and shoulders, he felt sure, for her makeup was fresh when she reappeared on the dance floor at half past twelve on the dot.

He sat hunched over his books all week, but as soon as the Fiday supper was done, he and Cardo boarded the street car and he danced the night away with the girl of

the rosy cheeks and red **lips**. He danced with her exclusively while Cardo distributed his dance tickets among the girls.

In time he got to wondering if it was because of his heavy library readings, but he saw his cheeks rather pale in the bathroom mirror. He regularly had a glass of milk at a corner stand on the way home from the library in the evenings, and this helped some but did not seem nearly enough.

About this time he saw a movie about a dead Transylvanian count who was entombed in his castle and one night each week came back to life, grew wings, and flew out. He then entered bedrooms in the countryside, stuck his tubular teeth into the necks of sleeping folk, and sucked their blood. He flew back into his castle before dawn, lay down in his coffin that was conveniently left unburied, and went back to sleep, apparently dead till he became thirsty for blood a week later and would then get out of his coffin and fly out on his weekly expedition to suck blood. Finally the creature was followed to his coffin, speared in the heart, and killed for good.

He looked up the subject of vampires in an encyclopedia and found that the belief in them was still common in the Balkans. There the medieval church authorities had authorized the periodic opening of tombs in cemeteries and the spearing of the hearts of corpses that seemed to have remained looking just asleep rather than in a state of decay.

His pretty dance partner promptly reappeared in the hall at half past twelve. She rose and clasped him when he strode to her as soon as the orchestra struck up and led him into their usual dark corner, pressed her tender lips to his neck, and said little or nothing the rest of the night.

He thought long about it, and after she left at twelve one night he discreetly followed her. He kept at a distance in the shadows and saw her take a small flashlight out of her bag and flash it on the ground as she rounded a grassy corner. Finding her gone when he turned the corner, too, he stood close to the trunk of a large tree.

Finally she came out, and he knew where to follow her the next time. He quietly walked back into the hall after her and they danced till near dawn.

He watched her turn off the street into a half-concealed alley when he quietly followed her the next week. She headed for a small cottage under an old mango tree a little apart from the other houses behind a tall hedge under which two cats, a contralto and a tenor, were doing a counterpoint. He saw her walk up three steps and then open and close a door. She flicked a switch and flooded the room with light. He then hurried toward the cottage following a narrow strip of light falling on a green leaf on the hedge just outside the wall of her cottage. The light, of course, had not been there before she switched it on.

He stepped to the crack in the wall through which the light emerged, peeped in, and saw her standing before a dresser and touching her cheeks and lips with rouge. Then she sprayed a scent on her earlobes, drew back a little, and stuck out her tongue at the mirror, and he suppressed a gasp at what he saw. Her tongue was half a span long out of her mouth. It was thin and tapering to a needle point moistly gleaming in the bright light.

She then quickly drew in her tongue, turned before the mirror, flicked out her sharp tongue again, glanced at it, and drew it in. Finally she picked up her wrap and bag, walked to the door, turned the light off, and shut the door after her.

He walked quietly a safe distance behind her and watched her return to the dance floor. Then he walked to Cardo and told him he was not feeling well and would like to go home ahead. He never went to the cabaret again.

He soon regained his weight and finished his course a semester ahead of schedule. For over two years he was jobless in that time of the big economic depression of 1929-39. He joined a band of homeseekers aboard a black ship to Cotabato to hunt for a job but found none there either. He landed his first job as an elementary school teacher at ₱45 a month back home in Luzon. Then he came out tenth in the senior teacher exams given by the civil service bureau and was sent to Cagayan High School, in Tuguegarao. The director of civil service in Manila maintained that he could get no more than ten percent more than his previous pay. Since that would upset the pay scale of the high school, the Cagayan schools superintendent abolished his item in the budget. He went home and a wire from the education director in Manila then came sending him to the Lanao High School in Dansalan, now Marawi City, where he started at ₱90 a month teaching English and history. After the highly capable J. Scott McCormick became schools superintendent for Lanao where he had been exiled by the new education director, Celedonio Salvador, and where he was until his transfer to Sulu where he was to be killed on the beach when he encountered the Japanese invaders, he was promoted in pay three times a year till his salary was ₱130 a month. Then he went to Mapa High School, in Manila, his wife having been confined at the Quezon Institute for pneumothorax treatment for three years, topped a civil service test in English, and went to Indiana University where he sat in a class under Stith Thompson, the famous folklorist, who was to lecture on the vampire as a folklore character.

IN EUROPEAN folklore, the vampire is a ghost said to suck human blood. A vampire left its grave or tomb in the dead of night once a week, usually on Wednesdays, sucked the blood of a sleeping person, and flew back into its coffin before dawn. The belief in vampires is widespread in both Asia and Europe but is most widespread in the Slavic belt. Articles and fiction about vampires continue to be published. A recent magazine story tells of an American tourist and her exuberant young daughter being squired around by a handsome young man in the Balkans. The girl grew paler and more emaciated as they did the tourist spots, and finally the mother decided that their guide was a vampire, dismissed him, and flew home with her pale daughter. The girl then rapidly regained her rosy cheeks and excellent health.

The belief in vampires has ramified to the medium-sized blood-sucking vampire bats of the Andes Mountain range in South America.

The names by which vampires are known to Filipinos include:

amalanhig — Hiligaynon

aswang as a blood-sucker—Bikol, Hiligaynon, Sugbuhanon, and Waray

Danag—Isneg

mandurugo—Tagalog

Philippine vampires are generally females.

A vampire flies out of her home at night and sucks out blood from people asleep other than the men they are married to so that they have a convenient home in the community out of which they can operate, as the viscera sucker who marries a human husband does, too.

Manuel and Lyd Arguilla tell a legend about a vampire loved by a village youth. She was "heart-melting in everyone's sight" and "her face had the beauty of flowers and the serenity of deep pools." She became a bride before she was sixteen.

The *amalanhig*—or *maranhig*—of the Hiligaynon is said to be a dead woman who has lived on because no one inherited her vampire state when she was dying. She lives in the woods, quietly enters villages at night, and sucks the blood of those asleep.

When about to die, a vampire asks a close relative to take over her vampirism. If no one agrees to do so, she lives on and remains a vampire.

One should climb up a crooked tree when pursued by the Hiligaynon vampire—the amalanhig—since her joints are stiff and she cannot negotiate the crook in the tree. If no crooked tree is around, one being pursued by her should follow a crooked path, for the vampire cannot follow such a path because she cannot bend her legs to turn. Or one should jump into a river or lake since an amalanhig fears bodies of water.

Bikol informants told Frank Lynch that the belly of an aswang gorged with human blood makes her look like a European vampire similarly filled with the blood it has just sucked as resembling a sack filled with grain.

Like the viscera sucker, as soon as the blood-sucking

aswang reaches the home of a prospective victim, it is said to alight on the roof, insinuates its threadlike tongue through a nipa shingle, and let it enter the body of a sleeper below. Like the viscera sucker's tongue, too, the Philippine vampire's tongue is pointed and hollow like a syringe and is thus adapted for sucking blood.

Bikolanos believe that like the viscera sucker, the vampire has a familiar sound that cries out "Kakak!" or "Kikik!" as the aswang goes through the air, whether, as variously reported, on wings, propelled by its ears or hair, or just like a rocket is not clear. Some say, however, that the sound is made by the vampire itself. As will be stated in the chapter on the viscera sucker, this writer has sometimes heard peculiar faint screeches coming from the sky on late nights. Ornithologists assure us that these sounds are made by wading birds flying out to other areas at night, but the folk feel sure they are made by the aswang.

Philippine vampires are said to live in their human husbands' homes, and this they can well do since they resemble good-looking women by day. The data yielded no information about Philippine vampires operating from graves or tombs as European vampires are reported to do.

Capiz is widely known to Filipinos to be where aswang—and in particular the vampire variety of the creature—are said to abound. Two field trips to Capiz made by this writer, however, yielded not a single report on local vampires—or viscera suckers either—and it is puzzling how the area acquired the unsavory reputation.

In their book Philippine Tales *and Fables*, Manuel and Lyd Arguilla tell a gripping legend about a pretty woman from Kalibo, Aklan—which used to be part of Capiz— who wed a sturdy youth. He wasted away and died before the year was out. She then married another healthy young man, and in turn he grew pale and thin and soon died. The same thing happened to her third husband.

A stranger spoke to her lusty fourth bridegroom and on his wedding night the latter kept himself awake after the lights went out. He heard her soft and even breathing

and almost abandoned himself to sleep. Then "he felt an oppressive presence hovering over him and a sudden prick at the base of his throat." He thrust a knife "into the bulk that he felt above him." There was a screech of pain and a flapping of wings, and next morning his bride was found dead below the window, a deep wound in her chest.

Zambales Ilokanos have no accounts about vampires and do not seem to believe that they exist. But they mention a mysterious nameless being said to enter homes after the members of the family have retired for the night and says:

> *Diak kayat ti nakinigid;*
> *Agallugit.*
> *Kayatko ti nagtengnga;*
> *Agammantika.*
> (I dont't want those at the edges;
> They smell of chicken droppings.
> I want those in the middle;
> They smell of lard.)

Two cultural overtones of this simple rhyme are of some interest. The lard referred to is pork fat and not vegetable oil which the folk consider far inferior to the former as food. Filipino families customarily bed down on a single large mat spread out at the center of the house which serves as the receiving room, sitting room, work room, kitchen, dining room, and bedroom. Fearful of vampires, viscera suckers, and other unwelcome intruders in the night, the children compete for the occupancy of the center of the mat. The chant discourages this preference and makes the borders of the large mat preferable as a sleeping place instead and their parents can then sleep together at the center.

The Isneg of Northern Luzon have a legend of how vampires learned to suck out human blood. Some Isneg folk once cleared their fields with their neighbors and planted them to taro. The forefinger of one worker was spiked with a splinter and a man sucked the wound, found the taste of the blood good, and sucked out all her blood saying it was sweet. The habit of sucking blood persisted.

The animal qualities of Philippine vampires are illustrated by the belief that fresh human blood is excellent for food. It is said that the small teats of vampires resemble those of most animals. An aswang is said to give suck to its children on her teats as small as cherries.

The magical character of the Philippine vampire is suggested by her ability to fly and by the report that she loses her supernatural powers with the first streaks of dawn or when she bathes in a stream and then rubs off the special ointment she has earlier rubbed on her body.

The Viscera Takers

The Manananggal
at a Teachers' Conference

A WEEK-LONG teachers' conference was held in Lucban, Tayabas—now Quezon Province—in 1930. Each town in the province sent delegates, and these were housed in the school buildings a kilometer from town.

The evening was dark when the delegates pulled in. The people living next to the school fence shuddered to hear the heavy flapping of wings and faint *tik-tik-tik* calls from the air. All were familiar with the belief that the mysterious calls of the *tik-tik* bird indicated the presence of the *manananggal* in a locality. This self-segmenter was a type of aswang said to enter a community at night, send down its immensely extendable tubular tongue from the roof of the house it perched on, and suck out the internal organs of a person asleep or an infant inside its mother in the house below. It was also said that the calls of the tik-tik were loud when the manananggal was far and soft when the monster was near.

The local citizens went to bed in great fear and woke up at dawn wondering what had happened during the night. They were relieved to find that nothing unusual had occurred.

The following night the men peeped out of their windows when they heard the sound of wings and the tik-tik-tik calls again. They saw dark, winged creatures flying over their roofs. The creatures had streaming long hair,

and their bodies extended no farther down than their waists.

"Manananggal!" they whispered to one another. They barred their doors and windows and had little sleep that night.

Those who waited on the delegates at the dining tables next day observed them closely. They saw a few of them pass up the spicy dishes such as *adobo* and *paksiw*, the first rich with spices and the second both spicy and cooked with lots of vinegar. Instead these guests ate lots of *dinuguan*—pork cooked with pig blood— and *inihaw-na-laman-loob*—roasted innards. The waiters looked at the armpits of these particular guests as they reached out for food in the platters. They had unusually deep armpits and did not look at people in the eye when spoken to.

The residents of the town hung sacs of crushed garlic, ginger, onion, and powdered black pepper at their doors and windows.

Restful nights returned to Lucban only after the conference ended and the manananggal left with the other delegates.

THE FOLLOWING are among the names of Philippine viscera takers:

    abat — Waray

    aswang that sucks internal organs—Bikol, Tagalog,
        Visayan

    boroka—Iloko

    manananggal—Tagalog

    mangalok—Cuyonon

There are numerous Philippine accounts about the folklore character known to Tagalogs as *manananggal* (self-segmenter or self-dismantler). The creature is called *aswang na lupad* (flying aswang) in the Bikol region and *boroka* —from the Spanish *bruja*, 'witch'—among the Iloko, who have probably forgotten its name in their native tongue although they dread the creature and have many legends about it. Whenever she heard strange screeches in the air at night, this writer's mother would throw salt and vinegar out of the window through which the sounds were coming and yell:

        "Asin, suka,
        Buroka, bakka!"
        (Salt, vinegar,
        Boroka, in a clay basin!)

There are no viscera suckers in European folklore nor in those of Africa and the Americas. But they abound in Philippine legends and in those of Indochina, Indonesia, and the long chain of islands extending almost up to Australia in the South Pacific.

The creature is said to resemble a ravishingly beautiful maiden by day and marries an unsuspecting man in order to live close to human communities. She goes to bed early with her spouse, and one informant from Samar reported that the creature quietly gets out of bed at moonrise, opens an eastern window, and stares at the newly-risen moon until her lower body drops off. In Southern Luzon and most of the rest of the country, what is said to be detached from her body is from the waist down, in Quezon Province from the knees down, and in most of the Visayan Islands and in Cambodia and Indonesia from the shoulder down, except that her internal organs go off along with her head and neck. She then propels herself through the air by use of her diaphanous hair or her ears.

She picks up the detached portion of her body and conceals it among the banana trees in the yard which it rather resembles in outline. Or she just leaves it where she lay beside her sleeping spouse and stretches out her bedsheet between her toes and her pillow to make him think she is asleep in her bed. Then she takes off, most informants say on wings and some say wingless like a sort of rocket. She cannot join her severed body if the part of it she left at home has been moved out of its original position.

She alights on the roof of the house she has quietly found to contain a likely victim, preferably a pregnant woman. Or, as Bronislaw Malinowski reports about the *mulukwausi* of the Trobriand Islands, she perches in a tree close to the village.

She then insinuates her enormously extendable tongue through a hole in the thatch and makes it float about in the room below like loose thread being blown about by the wind. It finally gets a lodgment in one of the ten bodily openings of the victim—the two eyes, two nostrils, two ears, mouth, navel, sex organ, and anus.

Dean C. Worcester, a zoology professor from the University of Michigan engaged in field work in Palawan toward the end of the Spanish regime in the Philippines, and later to become an energetic official in the Philippines under the American regime, reported in a subsequent book that the Balabac Island variety of the viscera sucker, called *balbal*, flew at night like a flying squirrel.

Viscera suckers are called *tanggal* ('segment') in Indonesia and elsewhere in Southeast Asia and are said to propel themselves with their hair or ears or, in Melanesia, with pandanus leaves.

Some viscera suckers sleep by day high up in tall forest trees, throwing their arms over a concealed top branch and draping their face with their long hair. Others live in isolated huts in the woods, perhaps several of them together, disguised as pretty girls.

A person becomes a viscera sucker after voluntarily swallowing a black, chicklike creature that pops out of the mouth of an old viscera sucker who cannot die and go to her final resting place or by unknowingly eating food licked by a viscera sucker. The mysterious chick is said to live in her stomach and feeds on the human entrails she has swallowed. The monster's craving for entrails is reportedly aroused when the chick starts cheeping.

Manuel and Lyd Arguilla retell a legend about a pregnant woman who one evening sat in her nipa hut sewing a layette for the baby she was expecting. She saw a length of crimson thread over her knees different from her thread. She looked closer and found that it stretched all the way to a tiny crack in the roof. She snipped it with her scissors and there was a shrill cry from the roof and a heavy thud on the ground. A strange woman was found dead under the window next morning.

Immediately after the viscera sucker's tongue enters the body of its victim, the monster sucks out the fetus or internal organs there. It then leaves, heavy with food.

Many countermeasures are prescribed against viscera sucker attack—an indication of how much the folk fear the creature. These fears help to account for certain

characteristics of Philippine culture and society and hence the usefulness of a study such as this.

The easiest way to kill a viscera sucker is to thrust the sharp end of a bamboo pole through her back. Boiled sliced tender bamboo shoots are a popular salad among Filipinos, perhaps because of the belief that the body scent this food gives those who eat it protects them from the monster. Bamboo is the most common building material in Philippine villages. The umbilical cord of a newly born infant is severed with a knife made from bamboo rather than with a steel knife or a pair of scissors even when these modern tools are more accessible. The ridge of the typical nipa roof in the villages is covered with a mat of bamboo slats held down by cruciform bamboo riders placed astraddle it. Since galvanized iron roofing is thought more secure against manananggal attack than grass or nipa shingles, this has become much preferred as roofing material even in the remotest villages.

The *banggera*, an open platform on which tableware, cooking utensils, vegetables, and the large clay jar where drinking water is placed to cool is open day and night to allow the air to freely circulate. It is floored with bamboo slats, is surrounded by a picket of bamboo sticks with sharp ends, and is thus believed effective in keeping viscera suckers away.

Among many Philippine groups there is a distinct fear of sleeping at the center of the floor or under a rooftree. This is because the viscera sucker's tongue is said to most likely drop to the center of the floor. Crossed bamboo staves with sharp ends are used as weights on the ridgepole of the roof since the Christian cross has, by a process of cultural accretion, come to be thought of as a countermeasure against viscera suckers alighting on the rooftree. Too, the folk believe that vampires, viscera suckers, and witches are easiest killed with sharpened bamboo thrust into their backs. Iron is also a countermeasure against these creatures, and the common use of sharp cones of galvanized iron at the gable ends of many a Philippine roof can be traced to the fear of these beings— plus the fact, of course, that this decor has an artistic function. Islam prohibits the display of graven images, but the beam-ends of many royal homes in Muslim Lanao and Cotabato are decorated with engravings of faintly disguised crocodile heads, and crocodiles are said to be feared by viscera suckers.

A Spanish chronicler reported that at the birth of a child in the Philippines, an adult male climbed to the roof at midnight, took off his clothes, and stood swinging his bolo about—a practice evidently meant to keep off viscera suckers. He stripped to show that he was male and could not be pregnant.

Villagers pull their sheets over their heads when they go to bed in spite of the heat and what they are told in school about the need for fresh air. And they sleep prone besides. Both customs are thought to minimize exposure of their bodily openings to the viscera sucker's probing tongue.

To the belief in viscera suckers can also be traced the large size and noise of the Filipino family. The more noisy the group to watch against these predators of the night, the safer life is thought to be.

The abundance of spices, salt, and salted fish sauce in Philippine cooking is traceable to the folks' belief that these keep viscera suckers away from what they eat.

This writer once had occasion to ask some Laguna de Bay fishermen to reproduce the call of the manananggal's scout, the *iki* (Tagalog) or *wakwak* (Visayan). This bird is said to reconnoiter at night above the roofs for its mistress, the viscera sucker, then at rooftop or ground level waiting for intelligence from its private detective. The calls of the scout are said to be loud when the viscera sucker is far from the intended prey and faint when near.

The fishermen replied that the call was too high-pitched to reproduce. This writer often hears sharp screeches across the sky on quiet nights from his country home in southern Zambales, and they would indeed sound scary to those inclined to believe that viscera suckers are real. He has even heard similar screeches right over his home in Quezon City, and he wonders why he had never heard them before. Perhaps it is true that those who believe in ghosts soon see ghosts.

In his Zambales home this writer has often heard the

sound of wakwak flying across the sky from the river
mouth to the southwest of town toward the marshy areas
at the foot of the mountains in the northeast at late hours.
The scientific name of one bird in Dioscoro S. Rabor's
Philippine Birds and Mammals (U.P. Science Education
Center, 1977) is Rufus night heron (*hycticorax caledonicus*
Vigors). Rabor describes it as a nocturnal bird which
spends the day at rest in swamp trees with thick foliage.
Rabor adds: "The harsh call of this bird sound [s] like
'wak-wak-wak . . . wak, wak, wak . . . ' given when
perching at night in a long harsh shriek that is hard to
imitate." That may well be the call of the manananggal's
reputed scout.

The manananggal that went to the Lucban ccnference
did not touch the adobo and paksiw served them because
the creature is said to loathe highly spiced dishes such as
these. The Filipinos' decided preference for salt, sour, and
spicy foods is likely due to their fear of the manananggal
and similar preternatural beings. That the manananggal
delegates in the above legend ate plenty of dinuguan
(pork cooked with pork blood) may, however, be a case of
what folklorists call function transfer. Instead of the
viscera sucker, the demonological being which the folk
believe to drink human blood is the vampire variety of the
aswang, called mandurugo ('blood taker') in Tagalog.
Philippine vampires today are said to suck blood out of
their dancing partners in dark nooks of night clubs,
making tiny pinpricks in their necks with their syringe-
like incisors and tongue-tips. Vampires are also reported
to own some of the blood banks in cities.

Philippine rural communities are endogamous. Village
boys tend to marry their next-door neighbors and cousins.
They prefer these to girls from outgroups, especially when
the latter are too good-looking. The consent of the bride's
or groom's elders is needed before a marriage can be
made. The prospective bride—as well as the groom—goes
through a rigid screening process by the grandparents,
uncles, and aunts, as well as by the parents before a
marriage is made. The yearlong free service of the young

man in the girl's home before marriage is still observed and it is likely that this is thought to allow the prospective groom to observe whether the girl he proposes to wed is not a viscera sucker. Such customs as these were probably born of the fear of men marrying glamorous girls from outgroups who may prove to be viscera suckers.

One gets to understand Philippine society and culture better by getting to know the legends Philippine folk tell about such demonological beings as the viscera sucker.

The Werebeasts

Sometimes a Dog

HE WAS LIKE any of his neighbors in the village by day and on most nights. He plowed and harrowed a corner of his field, made seedbeds there, and sowed the seed rice and let it germinate and grow. Then he plowed the rest of his field and left the plowed land idle while waiting for the monsoon rains to come.

The rains arrived when the seedlings were about knee-high. He then plowed his field anew, pulled out the seedlings, tied them in two-span bundles with bamboo strips, shook off the soil in a creek, and beat the bundles together two at a time to shake off the soil and loosen the roots.

Finally he harrowed the field and planted the seedlings in it.

He waited for the crop to come up, grow panicles, ripen, and be ready to reap.

He went to market with a shopping bag woven from strips of palm leaves and bought meat, fish, and fish sauce and greens and the other things he needed in his kitchen. He had his haircut every two or three weeks in a barber shop at one side of the town square. He seemed to be a happy bachelor without a care in the world.

But something unusual happened to him after supper on some nights during the month. He turned into a beast. An irresistible urge made him go down his ladder, leave his yard, and go out to find someone he could tear up with his teeth.

He tried everything he could think of to resist the peculiar urge, telling himself that it was cruel and inhuman. But he simply was powerless against it when it came.

He once took a bus to the big city. He went to a hospital and asked a doctor there what was wrong with him. The doctor made him lie down on a soft spring bed and examined him and said there seemed to be nothing wrong with him—he was, the doctor summed up, perfectly healthy.

He took the bus back to the country without a prescription for what was ailing him.

He then discreetly asked around the village what could be done to help a person—he made it a point to indicate that it was any man, woman, youth, or child— and he described what was troubling him. He gathered that such a person was an aswang, a word, someone added, probably short for *asuasuan*, a man who sometimes turned into a beast resembling a dog in appearance and habits. He also gathered that one became an aswang after eating human liver, perhaps in an out-of-the-way public eating place. There was no cure for an aswang, he also learned, and the only way to avoid the disease—for it was

a disease—was to avoid a restaurant if one was unsure of
what the meat being served there was.

He knew he was about to turn into an aswang when
his clothes started feeling loose on his body after dark. He
then quickly took his garments off, tossed them into a
drawer or under his bed, saw coarse hair start growing
over his face, neck, arms, body, and legs, and a tail began
to grow as a lower extension of his backbone.

Sometimes he felt the change coming on while walking
in a dark street or alley. He would take off his clothes,
leather slippers, shoes, or clogs—whichever he happened
to have on then—and quickly hid them in the shrubbery
or hedge by the road or street. He would then roam the
streets till about midnight, sniffing around for people to
attack.

He did not turn only into a dog. He turned into what-
ever was the first fierce animal he met on the street just
before he became a beast. He sometimes first met a hog
and then he became a boar with sharp tusks, a carabao
and he became a fierce bull, or a cat and he turned into a
ferocious tom. Animals he met in the streets seemed to

know he was an aswang and they quietly avoided him.
No dog, swine, carabao, or cat ever fought him. Only
people seemed fooled by his appearance as a domestic
animal.

He promptly became a man again after the midnight
bell tolled, and he quietly walked home, put on his
clothes, lay down in bed, and slept soundly till daybreak,
after which he rose and lived as an ordinary man.

This went on and on, and he could do nothing about it.
He grew old and died, happy that he could at last go to his
final resting place.

THE WEREBEAST is probably the most feared
demonological being in Philippine folklore today. The
corresponding creature in European traditional lore is the
werewolf, in the folk belief known as lycanthropy, a word
derived from the Greek *lykos*, 'wolf', and *anthropos*, 'man'.
The term *werebeast*, however, is more appropriate than
werewolf to designate the creature in Philippine folklore
since there are no wolves in the county, and besides, the
creature is widely believed to turn into any of various
ferocious—or potentially ferocious—animals such as the
dog, the pig, the carabao, and the cat.

The local names of Philippine werebeasts include:
aswang na lakaw ('walking aswang')—Bikol
kiwig ('sloping')—Aklanon
malakat ('walker')—Sugbuhanon

It may be that the belief in lycanthropy developed
from formerly widespread traditions in many countries
that men could actually assume animal shapes. A person
is said to take the form of the fiercest animal in an area—
the wolf in Europe, the leopard or hyena in Africa, and the
tiger or fox in India, China, Japan, and other Asian lands.
Thus, in addition to werewolves, there are wereleopards,
werehyenas, weretigers, and werefoxes in various parts of
the world.

The folklore of many areas contains stories of
lycanthropy. Arcadia, celebrated as the land of idyllic
peace in ancient Greece, was nevertheless plagued by

fierce wolves. The Arcadians believed in what they called
the wolf-Zeus, the supreme deity who combined the traits
of a wolf and an all-powerful human god.

The ancient Romans believed in lycanthropy, too. They
called a person thought capable of turning into a wolf by
use of magic spells or herbs *versipellis*-('turnskin').

Werewolf legends were commonly told in medieval
Europe, and bandits often took advantage of beliefs in
werewolves by wearing wolfskins over their clothes to
petrify their victims. Suspected lycanthropes were tried
and burned at the stake like witches when convicted.

Robert Louis Stevenson's *The Strange Case of Dr. Jekyll
and Mr. Hyde* is a supenseful novel about a werewolf in a
modern English city. The book is on the reading list of
Philippine schools and colleges and tells about a perfectly
nice urban medical practitioner whose shape periodically
alternates between a pesky wolf that terrorizes people in
the city and a pleasant urbanite in coat and tie.

Francis X. Lynch, a Jesuit who later assumed the name
of Frank Lynch, wrote *Ang Mga Asuwang: A Bikol Belief*, a
monograph on what Bikolano informants believe about
the aswang when he worked with the Bikol River Basin
Project before heading the Institute of Philippine Culture
at the Ateneo de Manila University. Dr. Lynch wrote that
a werewolf is a man who assumes the form of the first
animal he meets after coming out of his domicile at night.

Earlier Philippine sources such as the Philippine
Census Report of 1903 stated that the werebeast assumed
the form of any animal it might choose, such as a dog, a
cat, or a hog rather than what the creature first met when
going out on a prowl after dark, as in the legend this
chapter starts with.

Richard Arens, who was for a time on the Silliman
University faculty, did field work in the Eastern Visayas
on the side and reported that the *malakat* ('the walker') of
Leyte could be either male or female—something unusual
since the creature is said to be always male in other
reports. Arens described an attacking malakat in these
words:

In attacking a person, she assumes a horrible and frightful shape. Her long hair spreads all over her face. Her eyes turn fiery and her saliva flows from out of her mouth like long strings. Her nails grow long and sharp. As the fight begins, her hair crawls into the person's nose, ears, mouth, and eyes, depriving him of his breath, voice, and sight. She grips the victim firmly on the arms and legs. With her sharp claws, she digs into the victim's skin until it bleeds; if [she] has a weapon with her, she avoids the struggle and the victim might be killed; thereafter [she] feasts on the victim's flesh.

The Apayaos tell a legend about a woman who one afternoon went to gather greens in a field and met a large black dog with its tongue out. Thinking that it was thirsty, she called to it, and it suddenly turned into a dark, stange-looking man whose smell was so unpleasant that she threw up.

Like the Philippine witches, werebeasts are generally
reported to live in rundown nipa or grass huts at the
outskirts of communities and to look just like ordinary
village folk by day.

Like the demons of Philippine folklore, too, some
werebeasts change their shape at night before the
beholder's eyes. These shapes are those of vicious-looking
beasts. They are said to take the form of the animal they
first meet when going out on a prowl at night.

Werebeasts generally sleep all day after a night of
prowling. A werebeast is said to become ill if it fails to go
out on a prowl on the night it is scheduled to do so.

A report from the Camarines area states that the
aswang devours people and scours the streets at night
looking for people to attack. Most Philippine folk are
averse to going out of their homes after dark for fear of
werebeasts on the prowl.

An informant from Marikina, just east of Manila, said
that an aswang in the form of a dog was known to sit
sniffing at a street crossing in that town waiting for
prospective prey at night.

Benilda Moreno, this writer's former maid from
Baybay, Leyte, said that the segben looks like a white goat
with its posterior higher than its head and shoulders. She
added that the creature can run just as fast forward as
backward. She said that she once saw a segben eating
grass in her parents' yard, and the creature leaped over
the roof when it left. Visayans also call the creature
umatraka, able to go as fast backward as forward.

Village folk used to light their way with torches of
burning bunched rice straw, dry coconut fronds, or dry
bamboo sticks which they swung back and forth when
going out, usually to call for a healer after dark. Where
there is no electricity, today they use flashlights and will
often try to subdue one another with their electric torches
when out in the streets at night to prove how powerful
their equipment is.

One is said to be best protected when out at night in
the streets from werebeast attacks by carrying the tail of a

stingray or a rattan stick. The prickly tail of the stingray is commonly tucked behind the door above the ladder to keep werebeasts as well as other demonological beings such as demons, elves, viscera takers, and witches away. Mothers also place the ray's tail or rattan stick beside an infant asleep in its crib to ward off these demonological creatures. These objects can usually be seen lying beside a sleeping baby in its crib—bamboo since this cane is itself a protection against certain demonological beings—while its mother is at work in the kitchen or out in the yard.

Being human by day, a werebeast has human traits then. He performs his daily chores and interacts with people.

A weredog is reported to stop walking at once when called by the name of the man it is werebeasting for. Since the creature is a beast part of the time, it is said to behave like a beast then and bites and devours people as a carnivore does. In the late seventeenth century, Juan de Plasencia, a priest who labored in the Laguna area, listed what he called the eight "agents of the devil" which he identified as feared by the Tagalogs. He wrote: "The eighth they call asuang [*sic*]. . . . They say that he murdered men and ate their flesh. This was among the Visayas [*sic*] Islands; among the Tagalogs these did not exist." The Tagalogs did have similar beliefs, however.

Plasencia added that the mouth of the creature dripped when it attacked, and then it clawed the body of its victim. It entered gardens like an ordinary dog and ruined the plants there.

Some of the magical traits of werebeasts are indicated in Lynch's monograph on the Bikol aswang. He wrote that when the creature left its home in the form of a man to make his nocturnal rounds, it rubbed on its body a foul-smelling secret oil which then enabled it to "walk as swift as the wind, weaving in and out of housetops with the greatest of ease; but [according to] other informants, he automatically becomes this swift-moving and self-transforming when darkness comes on."

Lynch categorized the countermeasures against the

aswang as words from the scriptures, holy water, leaves
blessed on Palm Sunday, incense, and the crucifix. This
list, however, appears to confirm the warning that
informants tend to answer a researcher's questions in the
way they think the researcher would expect. The countermeasures reported by other researchers are more varied.

Also reported by Fr. Lynch as effective in keeping one
safe from the aswang when one is out walking at night are
the following: certain fruits, spices, seeds, leaves, kinds of
wood, and the fruits of certain plants, especially the lemon
and the kalamansi, which one should carry slices of and
rub on one's person when setting out at night. One should
also put slices of these fruit under a patient's mat or bed to
keep the aswang away. The wild eggplant, called *balballosa*
in Iloko and *talampunay* (*Datura metel* Linn.) in Tagalog, is
also reported to be especially effective in repclling the
aswang.

Shavings from carabao horns thrown into live coals are
also said to keep werebeasts safely distant. The leaves of
certain plants are burned in a slow fire under and around
the house in the evening to keep the aswang away.
Burning garlic also keeps the creature at a safe distance.

Bolos are inserted between the floor slats and left
hanging there at night so that the aswang will not go
under the house to wait for a chance to attack.

One report stated that a person set upon by an aswang
should stab the creature at the posterior. Then the aswang
is said to assume its human shape and thus becomes
relatively helpless.

A wounded aswang should be cut in two down its
spine and the halves should then be cast on the opposite
sides of a stream. In this way the halves cannot reunite
and the creature will die. This particular belief may have
been suggested by the European belief that witches are
afraid to cross the sea.

Philippine folk believe that a man may become a
werebeast in either of two ways—by inheritance and by
bodily contact with a werebeast through its breath, what
it eats, and what it drinks.

An ordinary person is said to be liable to turn into a
werebeast if a werebeast succeeds in putting a mysterious
chick into his mouth. After the person swallows the chick,
it will grow into a monster in his stomach and make him
crave for raw human flesh. This mysterious chick is said to
be capable of being expelled in either of two ways. One
way is to tie the patient to a swing, twirl the rope, and
sudenly release it. The patient will be dizzied and vomit a
black chick, and this should then be caught and quickly
thrown into the fire to burn.

The other way to expel the mysterious chick is to hang
the patient by the feet from a tree, light a pile of rice straw
under him, and let the smoke from the fire nauseate him
until he vomits the chick. When this happens, the chick
should be cast into the fire to prevent it from getting back
into the patient's mouth.

The Witches

A Varied Switching

A MAN SECTIONED three adjoining spans of a brown piece of bamboo into sticks. He cleaned each stick and sharpened it at one end. Then he drove the sticks into the ground around a yearling *malunggay* tree growing outside his wife's kitchen window.

He walked to a clump of droopy bamboo used for making rope and twine in a corner of his lot. He cut off three branches, split them, and carried them to the yearling tree. He then wove the splits around the sticks.

"No pig or goat will touch this tree again," he thought. "She will cook tender malunggay pods two harvests from now," he added, thinking of his wife.

An old woman with a stick came hobbling down the narrow street, a faded kerchief tied about her head. The sleeves of her brown bodice draped her arms, and her skirt had a design of gray squares. She lived in an isolated grass hut under an old tree at the outskirts of the village. People avoided her and storekeepers promptly gave her what she wanted to buy or have for the asking. No one knew her name, who her relatives were, or where she was from.

"Your tree will grow tall," she told the man as she passed by.

"It will, it will," he replied, looking at her with a frown.

A young man unhitched his carabao from his cart at
the roadside end of his rice field a day or two later. He
started reaping with a finger-long crescent steel blade
planted across a slender wooden stick he held in his fist
while he reached down for the rice heads and pressed
them with his middle and third fingers on the blade,
cutting them cleanly. He whipped the heads he cut into
his free hand at regular intervals and then pulled the
leaves from the fistful of heads, bound them with a
bamboo strip, put the bundle on the ground, and reaped
on.

Toward noon he took his shoulder basket and headed
for his bamboo-weir trap that stood across a creek flowing
across his farm. He came out of the trap with a wrist-size
murrel and a couple of climbing perches in his basket. He
then reached down to the bottom of the creek and
gathered a handful of the inch-wide foot-long leaves of a
pond weed. He also pulled out a handful of the creeping
herb—*papait*—the bitterness of which he relished eating
with rice after he boiled and seasoned with salted fish
sauce.

He dug a shallow well beside his cart and cut out
section from the low levee. He gathered some faggots
from under a tree, built a fire in the levee, and cooked his
food. Then he sat down to his midday meal.

The old woman of two days before came walking by
while he was at lunch. "Come and join me,
Grandmother," he said, smiling at her.

"No, thank you," she replied, looking sidelong at him.
"Eat well and grow big," she added and walked on.

The young man finished his meal, washed the utensils,
and reaped on.

At sunset he loaded the rice heads on his cart. He
hitched his carabao to the cart and was soon on the road
home.

He complained of a severe pain in his stomach when
he got home. The pain was worse after supper and he
moaned all through the night. He went to see a doctor in
the morning. The doctor asked him some questions and
then wrote out a prescription which he presented to the
druggist in a corner store. He paid for the pills the
druggist gave him, took some right there and walked
home. But the pain grew worse and he lay groaning in bed
all day. His father had to take his carabao to pasture.

At noon his mother went for a healer from the other side of town. He asked the young man what he had done the day before. He mentioned his day in the rice field and the old woman who passed by. "She told me to grow big when I asked her to share my meal with me," he said.

The healer nodded his head and asked for a broom made from coconut midribs. After it was given to him, he tightened the hoop of rattan around its base, poised it over his shoulder, and said, "Whoever you are, get out of this young man!"

He paused, and the patient groaned in pain.

The healer then hit him lightly with the broom. "I said get out of this young man," he repeated.

Nothing happened, and the healer hit the patient harder to the posterior.

"Please stop!" begged a woman's voice out of the young man's mouth.

"I will thrash you unless you leave this young man—and at once!"

"I will leave," said the woman's voice. "I am leaving now."

The patient quieted down and was soon asleep. His mother sighed with relief and gave the healer a couple of silver pesos as he left.

The young man drove to his rice field and resumed his reaping next morning. He felt all right the whole day, but when he drove home at nightfall, the pain in his belly was back. He groaned and twisted in pain all night.

His parents then realized that the witch—for they now knew it was a witch—had reentered the young man's body, and they decided to go and ask for the services of a more potent healer. The young man's father took a horse to the foot of a wooded mountain where another healer was known to live. He found the healer's hut, asked to be let in, and told the old man who opened the door about his sick son.

The old man nodded and pulled a yard-long whip from behind his front door. It was the bottom section of a piece of rattan, the stumps of the cluster of roots at its butt end still there.

The two men rode together on the horse back to where the patient lay twisting in pain. The healer brought out his whip, firmly held the patient by the wrist, and poised the whip over him. "Leave this youth's body at once!" he said sternly.

The patient groaned in pain but nothing else happened.

"I said leave this young man's body right away!" the healer repeated, hitting the patient's posterior with the rattan switch.

"Oh, oh!" came the old woman's voice out of the patient's mouth. "Don't! Please don't! Let me go!"

The healer let go of the patient, who then lay quiet on his sleeping mat and was soon asleep, his breathing quiet and deep. The healer thanked the patient's mother as she put four silver pesos in his hand. "Come back for me if the young man has a relapse," he said, mounting the horse behind the patient's father and riding home with the latter.

The young man drove to his farm, harvested more of his rice, came home, and ate supper with his parents.

They were awakened by his moaning in the middle of the night. He said he could not breathe, and his chest was painful.

His father mounted his horse and drove to the seaside village five kilometres down and asked around for the healer with the stingray's tail. He was directed to a small hut at the edge of the village. He cleared his throat at the door, was asked in, and when he entered he sat down and said he was in need of a healer who used a stingray's tail for healing.

An old man came out and asked him in. The father told the man about his sick son and how a broom and a rattan stick had been used to cure him without success. "I have heard of your ray's tail," he added. "Please come and heal my son with it."

The old man disappeared behind the door and came out with a gray whip covered with short spines and the shiny brass knob on its butt end gleaming.

The two men rode on the horse to town and were soon beside the patient's bed. The healer seized the young man's arm and poised the ray's tail over his shoulder. "I have you in my power," he said. "Get out of this young man at once."

There was a brief silence, and the healer hit the patient's posterior lightly with the ray's tail. "I said leave this young man right away!" he ordered.

"I will, I will!" the patient wailed in the same old woman's voice.

The healer laid on with the ray's tail even harder, repeating his demand.

"Yes, good sir, I am leaving!" said the old woman's voice out of the patient's mouth. "Let me go!"

In a moment the patient, his brow covered with sweat, grew relaxed and was soon asleep. The healer sat watching him for a while. Then he was given his fee of a handful of silver pesos.

As he was leaving, the owner of the yearling malunggay tree that grew too fast and then withered entered the house and whispered something in his ear.

"And besides," the healer then said, "I want you to restore the health of the malunggay that you cursed with nice words," said the healer.

"I will, sir!" replied the voice. "I will!"

The young man got up next morning feeling fine and became permanently well. The malunggay yearling soon developed new shoots, too, and have the man's wife tender leaves and foot-long pods to cook as greens in due season.

THE MOST COMMON names of Philippine witches are the following:
aswang as a hexer or vindictive person—Bikol,
    Tagalog, Visayan
barangan — Visayan

mambabarang — Bikol, Visayan
mamumuyag — Hiligaynon
manananem — Pangasinense
manggagamod — Iloko
mangkukulam — Iloko, Pangasinense, Tagalog

Witchcraft is the subtle exercise of what are claimed as supernatural powers for purposes contrary to social life. It is also known as black magic. A woman believed to have these supernatural powers is known as a witch if she exercises her powers without pay and a sorceress if she accepts a fee and can thus be considered a professional. The male counterpart of a witch is a warlock and that of a sorceress is a sorcerer.

The fear of witches still grips many primitive societies the world over and is common even in the most technologically advanced countries today such as those in Europe and North America.

A man shown with horns on his head is painted on the walls of caves in European archaelogical sites dating as far back as 3000 B.C. and in territories extending from Spain to Russia.

The belief in witches was widespread in England up to the eighteenth century, 1,200 years after Christianity reached that country. Beliefs in withcraft still exist in Europe today. Witch gatherings, called witches' sabbaths, are still regularly held in European countries throughout the year. Halloween in both Europe and North America on November 1 still features witches. In these, people in witches' clothing go around saying, as they still do in the United States, "Treat or tricks!" to people they meet in the streets after dark. Instead, on All Souls' Day, also on November 1, Filipinos build shrines for the dead at street corners and in the cemeteries they spend All Saints' Day Eve and all of the following day at the graves or tombs of their dead, remembering them and telling stories about them while they take their meals right there as well.

In his *Odyssey*, Homer tells about Circe, who bespelled and for years imprisoned Odysseus and his men in her cave by the sea, but she eventually relented and let them to. The legendary Medea was the most famous sorceress in classical antiquity.

The Fathers of the early Christian Church generally held that the belief in witchcraft had no basis in fact, though they admitted that mentioning the name of Jesus by a Christian believer was effective in countering an attempt to bewitch. This belief reached the Philippines while Spain occupied the country and has survived in the popular exclamations of *Susmariosep* in reacting to anything ominous or ever merely unexpected.

St. Augustine (354-420) had heard of Italian women innkeepers giving cheese to travelers who turned into draft animals after they ate it, and he expressed his strong disbelief in these stories. Nevertheless the belief in witches and witchcraft spread, perhaps because of the very preachings against them addressed to credulous unlettered folk who had never heard of them before.

There had been witch trials for almost a century before the Inquisition of Toulouse in 1335. The records of this inquisition tell of accused women confessing that they went to witches' sabbaths on Friday nights, had sexual intercourse with the devil disguised as a goat, cast spells, and committed acts of sacrilege at holy communion. They also confessed to brewing poisonous herbs with a philter of human and animal corpses and clothing from those who had been hanged, to the belief that the devil was equal to God and was the ruler of the world, to having made a pact with the devil, to making neighbors' crops rot, sheep sicken and die, and vineyards wither from frost, and to making people die by melting wax images attired in parts of their clothing. Many of these beliefs were to reach the Philippines through the Spanish missionaries, soldiers, and officials sent to the country during the almost four centuries of Spanish rule that began in the years when the fear of witches held Europe in its grip.

Joan of Arc (1412-1431), the heroine who liberated her native France from the British, was burned at the stake for witchcraft on May 30, 1431, and was made a saint by Pope Benedict XV in 1920.

Two Dominican priests—Henricus Institoris (Kramer) and Jakob Sprenger—wrote *Malleus Maleficarum* (1487), a detailed legal and theological treatise which Catholics and Protestants alike were to regard as an authoritative textbook on witches and witchcraft. A basic claim of the book was that witchcraft was due to "carnal lust" which certain women were said to be unable to resist. It also claimed that individuals accused of being witches should be investigated and where necessary tortured. Convicted witches, the book added, should be jailed for life and should be turned over to the authorities for execution if they did not repent. The usual method of exorcising the demon supposed to be in possession of the witch was to burn the witch.

Malleus Maleficarum was to profoundly influence all of Europe until the eighteenth century. Martin Luther (1483-1546), the vigorous leader of the Protestant Reformation, himself accepted the book as true.

Then came a slow change in the attitude toward the belief in witches. Paracelsus (c. 1490-1541) was among the first physicians to come out against the belief in witchcraft,

often at great risk to themselves, Giordano Bruno (1548-
1600), the Italian philosopher, wrote that many of those
claimed to be witches were merely psychologically
disturbed old women. St. Vincent de Paul (1581-1660)
denounced the belief in witches, too.

Another subtle type of witchcraft story illustrated by
the legend this chapter starts with was reported from the
East Visayas by Francisco Ignacio Alcina, S.J., in his
History of the Bisayas Islands (1668), translated into English
by Paul S. Leitz and published by the Universtiy of
Chicago in 1960. From the works of E.E. Evans Pritchard,
one sees that East African witches commonly use this
subtle type of witchcraft that is perhaps more suitable for
sophisticated reading.

Philippine witches are generally old men and women,
but there are far more women than men witches. They are
revengeful individuals who by magic or by a seemingly
innocent word or look, as in the legend, make people
seriously ill or die. In the Bikol area they also bewitch by
releasing a kind of beetle-like insects which they keep in a
bamboo tube hanging outside their window. Beside the
bamboo tube by day they hang a piece of clothing or other
personal belonging which they secretly took from the
intended victim to familiarize the agent insects with his
body scent.

Ilokano witches are commonly said to inflict witchcraft
by pricking with a needle a rag doll which they keep
concealed when not in use in the cylindrical compartment
that supports the portion of the common clay stove where
the fire burns.

Unlike the European witches, Philippine witches have
never been reported to eat human flesh. They are shy and
live in rundown huts at the outskirts of towns and
villages. They are said to avoid looking straight into the
eyes of people since one's being a witch can be seen in
their eyeballs, the image there being upside down, and the
eyeballs of witches are also said to be narrow and long like
those of cats and house lizards in sunlight. This particular
belief is behind the evasive glance of Filipinos—unlike

Westerners, for instance, who habitually look people
straight in the eye when spoken to. One can tell if a person
is a witch, it is said, by the shape of his eyeballs. Hence, if
one looks at another directly in the eye, one can be
suspected as trying to figure out from the shape of his
eyeballs if he is a witch—with dire consequences if he
proves to be one. Just the suspicion of witchcraft is
thought sufficient provocation for the witch to hex him
who suspects.

There are numerous ways thought effective in fighting
Philippine witches. In his study of Bikol witchcraft, Lynch
categorized these as certain plants, the smoke of certain
burning objects such as rubber, plastic, and the carapaces
of crabs and lobsters. Witches are also said to fear certain
rituals, certain objects commonly found in the home such
as coconut-midrib brooms, rattan canes, the sting ray's
tail, and dried peculiar-looking fish such as the globefish
and porcupine fish hung over the windows. One entering
a Philippine village, especially near the sea, is likely to see
these objects prominently displayed outside the windows.

Beliefs about witches have resulted in the average Filipino's compulsive fear of bugs that, attracted by the night, enter homes after dark, especially grasshoppers, moths, and mantises—and more of these creatures enter Philippine homes than in the West since few Philippine windows are screened. Filipinos swat these creatures heartlessly. It would be helpful if they feared the anopheles mosquito that spreads malaria with its sting at night too, but they have no such fear of this blood-sucking carrier of malaria.

Poor and deformed strangers are unwelcome in Philippine neighborhoods since they are feared to be witches. The general lack of sympathy for waifs and strays among Filipinos is traceable to their suspicion that these may be witches. This accounts for the existence of numerous legends about Christian saints who in the Philippines enter communities as beggars and punish those who deny them food or shelter—narratives likely invented by missionaries to counter the Filipino's hostility toward strangers. The disastrous effect of this trait on

social mobility is evident. The poor and underprivileged have little chance of improving their social standing.

There is, however, marked politeness to poor strangers when these cannot be avoided. For if one hurts the feelings of a vendor or peddler who proves to be a witch, the witch's wrath will be swift to fall.

For all this, however, the behavior of Filipinos toward witches is mild in comparison to that of the technologically developed Westerners.

Witches are said to inflict their witchcraft by uttering spells over something closely associated with the victim, such as his clothes. By magic they send tiny objects into the body of their victim, and insert these objects into the victim's body by use of insects the witch sends out to do this. One suffering from a disease otherwise impossible to explain, such as continuing nightmares and persistent psychological distress, may wonder if he has not seen witches, or his relatives may suggest this to him. And an individual who fears witchcraft may at first have none of the bodily symptoms claimed for witchcraft but the fear of a witching may lead to his developing these symptoms. This power of suggestion also helps to explain the reported phenomenon that a bewitched person speaks in the witch's voice when interrogated by the folk healer.

Philippine witches are said to look sickly and have red eyes by day but promptly become vigorous and active after dark. The toes of the Bikol witch are reportedly turned upward. Like some Visayan elves, some Visayan witches also have no philtrum. Donn and Narriet Hart wrote that like some West Visayan elves, witches have transparent throats and their food and drink can be seen going down their esophagus. Tagalog and Pampango witches are said to be either male or female, but early in this century Ethel D. Nurge wrote that the witch aswang was mostly female.

Philippine witches avoid human company and live in rundown isolated huts at the outskirts of communities to avoid interacting with people. The Harts wrote that a number of witches reportedly lived just outside Barrio

Lalawigan, in Samar. Lynch noted that the town of Iroga was traditionally known to abound with witches. Arens noted that the Visayan Islands are in Philippine folk beliefs the home of witches. From the abundance of witch lore in the rest of the country, however, one is hard put to avoid concluding that the entire Philippine archipelago can be said to be the home of witches.

It is reported that witches are most active at moonrise and moonset. Since dwarfs are reportedly around in people's yards at sundown, demons are in large trees and wander about in villages at night, and werebeasts are about after dark, it is little wonder that few Filipinos go around in the outlying villages between sunset and sunrise.

Reporting on the intellectual activities of Bikol witches, Lynch noted that witches avoid neighborhood social gatherings "such as the women's group at the river come together for washing, bathing, and exchanging small talk or the men's usual gathering at some favorite store or barbershop. They seek solitude and are given a wide berth by all."

At night the aswang are said to shun all light except that of the moon, and they are happiest when the moon is just starting to round.

Witches are usually respected because feared. They keep away from social groups by day but are amiable to people who befriend them. They are not quarrelsome and do not complain or seek people's advice. Some witches are said to go to mass and even take communion, but they look down instead of up at the host when the priest raises it. Thus, one way to detect witches is to look at what the worshippers do when the host is raised during mass. This reminds one of Wayland D. Hand's remark at a class lecture that the European witch alternately looks back to her left after she takes three steps and to her right after she takes three more.

The gifts that Philippine witches give to people, especially food, are politely accepted, burned, buried, or thrown to the dogs. This writer recalls that the pretty

young wife of a schoolteacher uncle was from the
northeast corner of the town, then as now known as the
home of witches. The uncle built his house in a corner of
the family lot. After the couple moved in, the bride one
day sent this writer's mother a cut of beef—a rare gift
since beef was dear and was never served at the family
table. This writer was astounded to hear his mother order
him to throw the meat to the dogs and indignantly
insisted that he do so when he tried to reason with her.
The couple eventually migrated to Cotabato after World
War I.

The magical power of the Philippine witch was
adduced in the C. R. Boxer Codex of 1590, which stated
that among the Visayans there were axuanes (aswang) or
malaques (*malakat* or walking aswang) who could kill "by
only saying that these persons they want to kill will die.
They say these can likewise kill any person they dislike
merely by looking at them."

Jose Nuñez wrote in *El Renacimiento Supplement* (Dec.
9, 1905) that by merely wishing it, the mangkukulam can
give anyone who has offended him an intense headache or

aches in other parts of his body, boils, tumors, or any other
bodily swellings. Nuñez added that a mangkukulam had
an *abubot*—a rattan basket with a lid—and when he had
planned to inflict harm on anyone, he went to where he
kept the abubot, took out a doll and a pin from it, and
stuck the pin into the part of the doll where he wanted his
victim to be stricken. The victim then became sick in that
part of his or her body.

The Batangas governor and supervisor of the 1903
Philippine census reported that the mangkukulam was a
man or woman who could make anyone he or she was
displeased with sicken or die. As a result, few had
anything to do with the mangkukulam and did everything
to please her.

Juan de Plasencia reported in 1589 that the *hobloban*, a
Catanduanes witch, had more power than the
mangkukulam, a sorceress. She could kill by just raising
her hand and could destroy the house of whoever
displeased her.

What can one do to counter a witch? Emeterio C. Cruz
learned from Filipino workers in Alaskan fish canneries
that a bewitched person should see a witch doctor who
had the necessary *anting-anting*, an amulet with
supernatural powers. The witch doctor's services were
free since he would be ineffective if he charged or
accepted a fee—in other words he was not a sorcerer.

In *A Visit to the Philippine Islands* (1859), John Bowring,
an Englishman who was in the country in the middle of
the nineteenth century, wrote that an explosion from a
bamboo cannon near the head of a bewitched person was
an effective cure for what was ailing him. The extensive
firing of bamboo cannons and the setting off of
firecrackers on New Year's Eve each year is contrary to
law but goes on unabated because of the belief that noise
from such explosions will banish witches for the rest of the
year.

Lynch's list of countermeasures against the aswang
among the Bikolanos is easily recognizable as European
and particularly Roman Catholic in origin. He wrote that

these included holy water, palm leaves blessed on Palm Sunday, incense, and a display of the crucifix. He also reported as effective the *oracion*, a mix of Latin words and phrases from a missal or other church text—for example, *Dominus spiritu cum vobisum fratres tuo*. He added that the oracion is written down on a piece of paper or in a little book and then carried as a weapon against the aswang and other demonological beings. An oracion recited in or under the house of a patient suffering from witchcraft is said to keep the aswang away.

Also reportedly effective in keeping the aswang away when scattered around the house are the seeds of the wild eggplant locally known as *talampunay* (Datura metel Linn.) and the leaves of the wild taro *gabi-gabi* (*Bootia reniflora* Merr.)

The smell of burning talampunay leaves, chicken feathers, leather, and now rubber and plastic as well, is said to keep witches safely distant. A slow fire under the house or window and fish hooks and bolos suspended between the floor slats are said to be effective in keeping the aswang away.

The Arenses wrote that bamboo spears and sharp knives suspended point down between the slats in the bamboo floor were effective in keeping the aswang away. So, too, are coconut oil made on Good Friday, table salt, ginger, and garlic. The pungency of garlic is said to be offensive to the aswang. Babies and children commonly have small pouches containing these items pinned on their clothes or tied around their necks or wrists for this purpose. A national interscholastic meet in the Visayas was almost canceled some years back when the members of a Southern Luzon delegation arrived with such pouches pinned on their shirts.

Edilberto P. Dagot reported that the countermeasures against witches in his native Cuyo, Palawan include ashes sprinkled on the doorstep, lemon, garlic carried on one's person wherever one goes, brass, copper, burning hoofs of cattle or swine, chicken feathers, hair, and a pestle placed across the doorway. The Cuyonon also believe that a live crab buried under the house of a witch will drive her away.

One report has it that the wound made on the animal form of a witch will show on the witch when it resumes its human form. It is also said that the aswang can reduce itself to near invisibility after she rubs a magic oil on her body while remaining extremely strong, slippery, and agile.

Frederick Starr's *A Little Book of Filipino Riddles* (1908) contains a Filipino riddle about the banana blossom which comes out of the top of the stem instead of from its side. It goes this way:

> *Nanganak ang aswang,*
> *Sa tuktok nagdaan.*
> (The aswang gave birth,
> It came out of the top.)

Lynch reported the belief that an aswang passed on her witchcraft by heredity. Two informants from Iriga, Camarines Sur, told his researchers that the aswang nature is passed on by simple heredity for seven generations.

It appears that witches fear unsightly creatures, unsightly though they themselves often are. In a Pampango folktale about "Juan Wearing a Monkey's Skin," the hero, clad in a monkey's skin, met three witches. "Now," says the tale, "witches are said to be afraid of ill-looking persons, although they themselves are the ugliest beings in the world." The witches were frightened off by his attire.

Dark colors, on the other hand, seem to fascinate Philippine witches. Black cats, large flies, and certain black night birds are said to be the messengers of witches.

In exorcisms of witches, the witch herself rather than the victim feels the pain inflicted, as in the legend this chapter starts with. Manuel and Lyd Arguilla illustrated this point with "The Pot of Boiling Water" which tells of a beautiful but proud virgin who became ill and died. Her body was dressed in her prettiest clothes and laid in a coffin with white wreaths proper to a pretty young virgin.

All admired her lifelike beauty when, as is customary in the Philippines, her coffin was opened for a last look at the burial pit. An old man who went there told the mourners that the girl was not dead and should be carried back home. The folk replied that to return the dead home would cause bad luck, but the girl's mother insisted that they carry her back home, and this was done. The old man then poured boiling water on the corpse. She sat up alive and unharmed and asked whether she had been asleep and why there were so many people in the house. Then the men sent out by the old man came back and said there was lamentation in the house of the mangkukulam, for his oldest son had just died from scalding. The son had been one of the girl's suitors.